Emotional
Anatomy

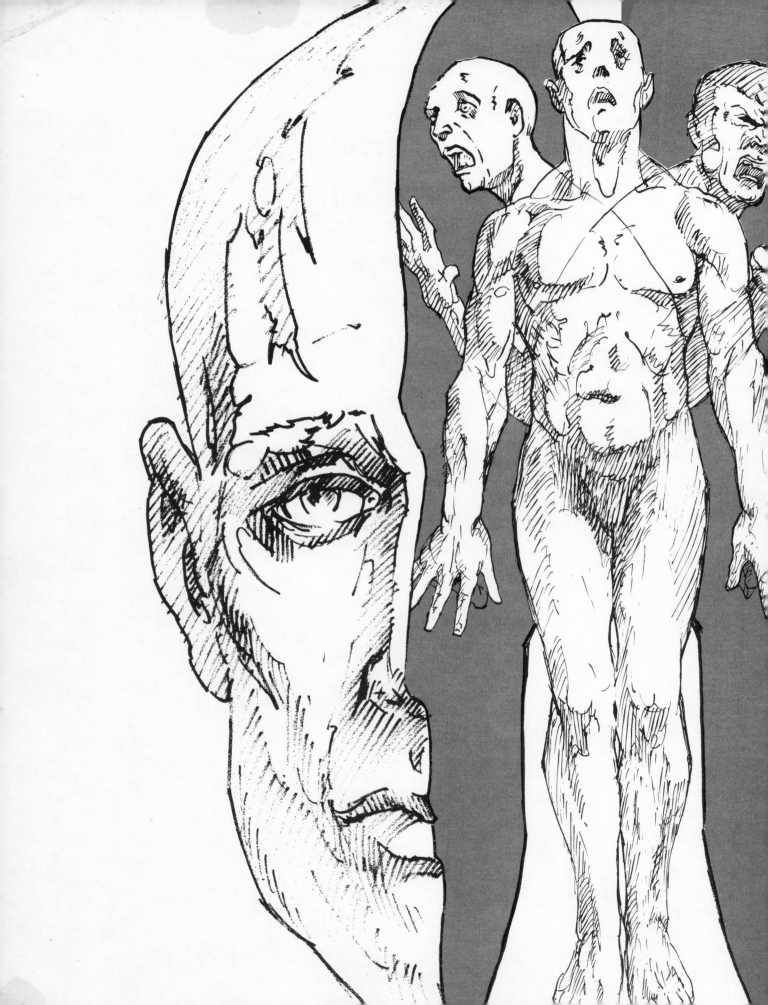

Emotional Anatomy

the structure of experience

Stanley Keleman

center press, *berkeley*

Published by Center Press
2045 Francisco Street
Berkeley, California 94709

Library of Congress Catalogue Number: 84-072535
ISBN 0-934320-07-1

Designed by Randall Goodall

to Gail

acknowledgements

To John and Ana Koehne and the Dharma Center, Shipman, Virginia, my gratitude for the generous grant that made this book possible and for their trust in my vision.

To Vincent Perez of Alameda, California, who illustrated this book, my respect and admiration for his exceptional talent and his ability to give artistic form to my original drawings and concepts.

To Gene Hendrix, Ph.D. of Berkeley, California, my special thanks for joining with me in forming this book, for his original contributions about its organization and themes, his consulting talents, his outstanding work as editor, and the many sacrifices he made.

contents

"You see I believe in shapes. I believe everything good has a shape. Shapes are the way in which we know who we are and where we are in our universe. Show me the shapes and forms a man gives to his life, and I will tell you whether he is a master or victim of that life."
—Gail Godwin
Glass People

introduction

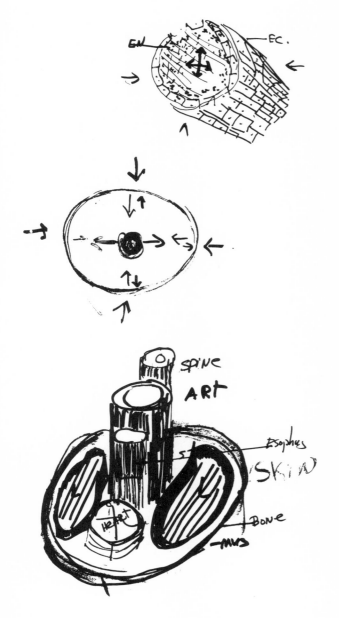

Life makes shapes. These shapes are part of an organizing process that embodies emotions, thoughts, and experiences into a structure. This structure, in turn, orders the events of existence. Shapes manifest the process of protoplasmic history finding a personal human shape—conception, embryological development and the structures of childhood, adolescence, and adulthood. Molecules, cells, organisms, clusters, and colonies are the beginning shapes of life's movement. Later on, a person's shape will be molded by the internal and external experiences of birth, growth, differentiation, relationships, mating, reproducing, working, problem solving, and death. Throughout this process, shape is imprinted by the challenges and stresses of existence. Human shape is marked by love and disappointment.

This book is a visual introduction to the shapes of human existence, the images and layers of life. From a process viewpoint, life is shapes moving somewhat like a movie. As movement slows, we can become aware of changes that occur in emotional posture from one moment to the next. If we could photograph our lives and show them frame by frame, we would see that we are moving sequences of varying emotional shapes. An implosion of cells organizes a fetus, then it shapes itself into an infant and, finally, into an adult. This journey of a fertilized egg organizes subdivisions, compartments, passageways, and labyrinths containing electrified fluids. As we dialogue with the shapes of our surround—first, the womb, then our mother, then many others—we form the strata of emotional shapes. This geometry of somatic consciousness finds visual expression in the images that follow.

During the last thirty years, in exploring emotions and the soma, I have understood what Freud stated so eloquently—anatomy is destiny. Anatomical process is a deep and powerful wisdom giving rise to internal feeling images. Outer body and inner organ shapes speak to us as cellular motility, as the organization and movement of psyche and soul. The feelings these shapes generate are the ground floor of brain programs, consciousness, the way we think and feel. Feelings are the glue that hold us together, yet they are based upon anatomy. This book visually depicts the archetypes of our inner and outer life and shows the essential dance of excitement and emotion as shapes of experience. From these somatic shapes we know genetic, social, and personal history.

Emotional anatomy is layers of skin and muscle, more muscles, organs, more organs, bone, and the invisible layer of hormones, as well as the organization of experience. Anatomical studies tend to depict images that are two-dimensional, thus missing the most important element, emotional life. At the same time, psychology, which is committed to the study of emotion, lacks an anatomical understanding. Without anatomy, emotions do not exist. Feelings have a somatic architecture.

In speaking about emotional anatomy, it is important to avoid concepts based on either what is "normal" or what is ideal. There is no ideal structure for humans. The primary concern should be how an individual uses himself to function. All humans stand upright but individuality is found in the variety of shapes and postures they assume. Therefore this book's images and story portray the structure of individual experience.

This book is organized like humans, in layers. There are six sections in the drama of existence. Chapter One—Creation—introduces the organizing process, embryology, the creation of internal space, the formation of layers, and internal relationships. Tubes and passageways organize from liquid life and set the stage for animate consciousness. In Chapter Two—The Body Plan—the plan of creation finds fulfillment as the adult human form. Tissues divide according to function, making layers that connect us, move us, and inform us. From these layers the ground of emotional knowing unfolds. Chapter Three—Insults to Form—shows that uprightness, the mark of human development, is altered by insults, challenges, and assaults. Given shape is changed by a person's emotional history. Chapter Four—Patterns of Emotional Distress—is the story of how each individual's shape reflects genetic emotional inheritance in interaction with societal "shoulds" and personal ways of self-organizing. Adults maintain a biological history as they create a personal existence. Each person's response to the world marks him, creating his unique emotional shape. This shape gives rise to individual consciousness. Chapter Five—Somatic

Reality—presents the complex layering of individual shape and gives suggestions for somatic education and reorganization. The last chapter—Somatic Interactions—shows how individuals move into the world to form a variety of relationships for cooperation, love, intimacy. Human community becomes a dance of the shapes of human interaction.

In this book, images are the primary teachers. They are meant to invoke and evoke, to be meditations that open the door to somatic emotional reality. Images of stress and challenge predominate, indicating how human form is primarily shaped. Life's challenges and a person's response to them create the shape he uses to express feelings of excitement, assertion, love, caring, and sexuality.

Emotional anatomy is somatic education, a tool to learn the geography and the archetypes of personal history. Emotional anatomy shows the relationship between shape and the genetic and social forces that inhibit or facilitate the shaping of a life. The experience of complex emotional patterns as somatic configurations gives a basis for living a richer somatic and emotional life. Emotional anatomy contains ancestral and ancient mysteries, present challenges and pleasures, as well as a peek into the future.

A forthcoming book, *The Formative Process: The Stages of Organizing Experience*, presents the remedial and educational aspects of somatic process work. Together, these two books establish the basic foundations of somatic process education, a modern contemplative approach.

These drawings are examples of Stanley Keleman's first sketches from which this book was prepared.

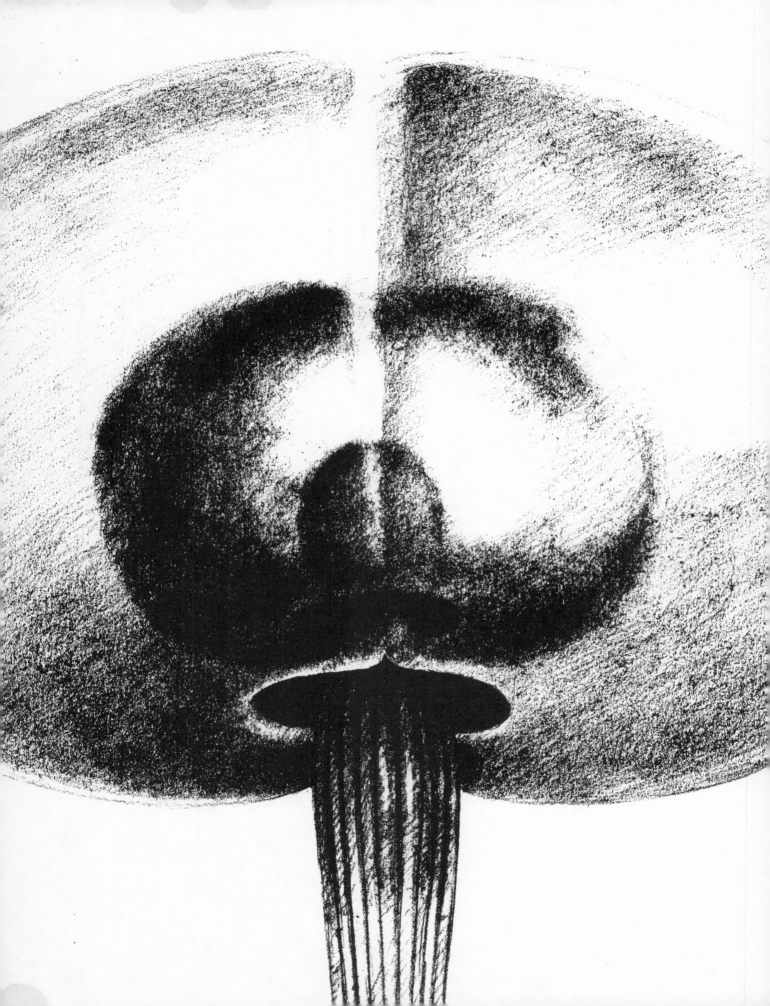

one

creation

EXISTENCE IS A tribute to how life organizes living forms. To be an individual is to follow the urges of one's own form, and to learn its unique rules of organization. This principle of organization, this imperative to form, is the language of the universe, society, and ourselves.

Life on every level is a process—a connected chain of separate living events that differentiates into specific forms of existence with an underlying theme. The universe is a process, a gigantic organized event of existence containing micro-organization. Society, likewise, is a process, a form that contains living subparts. And each of us is a process, a whole made up of living events with an urge toward organization.

This urge toward organization and form is what this book is about. How this urge or principle expresses itself in humans is depicted both in pictures and text. The starting point is the observed truth that the human form as a whole is made up of living events just as the universe is made up of living sub-systems. The process of creation is explored from its micro to macro development, from the exfoliation of a small event through its organizing ever larger and more complex layers of existence. From this view two facts are central: that life is a whole event and not a series of sub-systems, and that all life is inter-connected, springing from a common single matrix. Existence and organization proceed from outside in, from big to small. Events can be organized from outside in, as well as from inside out, from small to large, from general to particular events, or vice versa. Form has an organization and this relationship of form and function is the subject of this section.

Each life is a process. This process is universal. It is the nature of existence on our planet. It has, if not a determined order, an orderliness and a stabilized predictability and reliability which we recognize as the life of the species, the life of a specific animal, the life of a society or the biosphere. Each person's life as an organism within the planetary organism is a series of living events linked to create a highly complex form. In other words, each of us is a chain of living events, an organized network, a micro environment making a macro organism. From this point of view, the body is a living, organizing process that feels and cogitates about its own on-goingness and form.

Humans organize around a series of spaces. These spaces permit liquids to pass through. An early film on protoplasm by William Siefritz Ph.D. points out that cytoplasm and protoplasm organize a space by compression of outer boundaries and expansion of inner layers—whatever is moving creates a surface pressure that generates a passageway for itself from itself. From the motility of human fluids come the boundaries that are the body's own channels and tubes.

Man is a self-making organism. He is a series of organized spaces that develop a structure for nutrients and substances to move through. This structure of interconnected tubes moves vapors and gases. We process these liquids and gases to fuel our metabolism. Liquids pass through us, the nutrients kept and the dangerous or useless expelled. We bathe ourselves in a sea of liquid to exchange nutritional chemicals and give back to the world what is transformed.

Likewise we take in emotional nutrition from the world around us, use it for nourishment, and exchange with others what we have formed. We exchange germ cells and experience as well as carbon dioxide and oxygen. Motile passageways and tunnels give us an inside and an outside. These passageways contain spaces for specific activities like the kidney to transform serums or the mouth to masticate food and chemically break it down. Different spaces or pouches have different functions—the stomach is different from the lungs. Yet the pouches are specialized and localized units of generalized functions, lungs-respiration, stomach-digestion, brain-information.

It is the nature of these tubes and their corresponding pouches to have a particular kind of motility or peristalsis that transforms what passes through them. This particular pulsatory pattern organizes tissues into pumps. One of the fundamental elements seen in living material is its pulsatory organization, its ability to expand and contract, to lengthen and shorten, swell and shrink. This cellular movement of the cytoplasm and nucleus is seen in the internal movement of feeding and replication as one nucleus begins to stretch itself out and then congeal itself to form two daughter cells. This lengthening and shortening, this pumplike action, is a particular pulsatory pattern that is both similar and unique in all the various types of tissues. In cardiac tissue there is an uninterrupted rhythmical flow as compared to the expansion-contraction cycle of smooth muscle or the controlled interruption of lengthening and shortening of striated-volitional muscle or skeletal muscle. We experience the pulsatory beat of the heart and the quality of its rhythmical pattern. The heart's action, when it is excited or at work, can make us scared or cautious. Brain tissue also pulsates; it swells and shrinks as do the intestines. The whole organism is a pulsatory pump.

The organism is space with a structure. Seen as a pump organizing a series of spaces, the organism is tubes with layers. The organism, in fact, is a series of tubes and layers—neural, skeletal-muscular, digestive. This tube form is easily seen in cross sections—in the vascular tree, in the neural tree, in the digestive and liver track. These tubes are layered from the outside in—protective tissue, then a membrane, then a muscular layer, then more connective tissue, then a specialized layer around the lumen of the tube. Moving from inside out, there is first a delicate lining, endothelium in which substances are processed, then the supportive structure of the muscle, then fibrous tissue, and finally, another membrane. So there are major layers in every tube—an inside, an outside, a middle, and what is carried through the tube. Applying this principle to the entire body, the organism becomes a series of special layers that permit expansion and contraction at certain frequencies and amplitudes for the circulation of fluids, gases, ions. Just as brain pulsations maintain pressure to circulate cerebrospinal fluid, so does the diaphragm function to support internal pressure for the exchange of gases.

Tubal motility establishes each person's ongoing form and provides his basic feeling of identity. His pattern of expansion and contraction organizes basic perception and cognition—empty, full; slow, fast; expand, withdraw; engulf, disgorge. All feeling and thinking is based on this pumping action. This motility pattern can be exaggerated in overactivity or stilled by underactivity through fear, anger, or shock. We whip ourselves up until we are in a frenzy or we talk and feel ourselves into apathy and collapse.

Illustrations in this chapter show how spaces, tubes, and motility develop from a single cell; how a single cell has all the elements of expansion and contraction; how expansion and contraction organize internal space; how a cell produces swelling and shrinking; how one cell creates a series of cells and the organization of a tube; how one tube becomes two and two become three until we have a series of tubes; how these tubes are first organized horizontally, then vertically, and finally circumferentially; how these tubes organize themselves in the field of gravity; how a tube's verticality builds volume and assists in the passage of materials; how these tubes, their motility, and their spaces represent how we function and how we feel. A rigid tube leads to inflexibility, and feelings of self-righteousness and fear of collapse. A dense tube experiences little movement and brings fears of eruption; a swollen tube a lack of identity; and an empty tube feelings of longing and fear of assertion.

The history of the developmental organization of tubes, spaces, and motility gives a sense of how we function, what our insides feel like, and how we feel in general. Motility and movement display one pattern under distress, and another when we are in normal situations. These images of anatomy and feeling are presented from the inside out. What happens from the inside when we are emotionally and psychologically stressed? What happens to our tubes? What happens in the relationship of the pouches of our tubes to the other tubes that surround them? How do we organize ourselves for protection? Fight or flight, collapse or rigidity? How do we become overbound and thickened or underbound and porous? How do these states affect our connections to others?

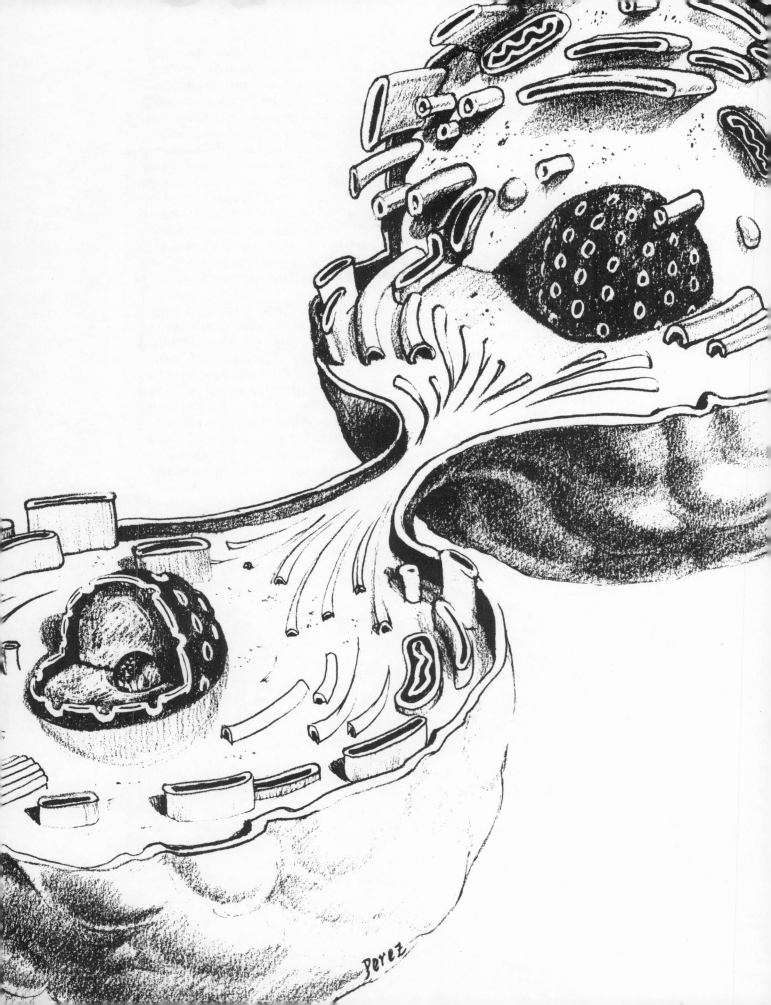

cells to tubes

The cell is mostly water in different states, polarized and pressurized as gas, vapor, lipid, and protein. It is changeable in shape; it rises and falls, coagulates and runs, collects and rests. This pulsation is contained within an area of cell membrane as well as by the micro-tubule-like pathways within the structures of the membrane. Cells transport substances and nutrients in special liquid-like steroids, or protein hormones. The expansion and contraction of tubal water and its derivative cells and tubes is central to the organization of soma, intelligence, and character. At our core we are liquidity in partnership with its vessels and its tubes.

The cell pulsates horizontally, vertically, and circumferentially. Cells stretch, lengthen, polarize, and divide their contents into equal parts, through a series of tubes, a line of force to make daughter cells. This division forms circular spheroid colonies, which form planes, plates, and then tubes. An organism increases in population from a single plane to layers and layers, becomes dense like city streets or high rise apartments.

In early embryological stages, all cells are directly connected, not yet separated by layers. Cells telegraph their condition directly and quickly through pulsation patterns and the liquid media they live in. Their connection and forms set up a common language, a harmony of pulsation that reflects their state of growth, metabolism, and the nature of their structure. All embryos, fetuses, and newborn children are closer to fluid tissue than they are to densely packed or calcified liquid.

Complex growth occurs through multiplication, densification, layering and then cell specialization into such components as heart muscle or bone. With the development of tubes and their pouches, pulsation begins to take place vertically as well as horizontally and circumferentially. This new step permits anti-gravitational organization. To prevent collapse and ejection of our internal contents, expansion and contraction need support. Chambers and valves are needed to maintain the peristaltic rhythms against the forces of gravity.

This is our metamorphosis from rhythmic pulsating cells into a multi-rhythmed pulsating organism. This organism is capable of functioning with dissonant, asymmetrical patterns. These appear as one pattern through the integration of complex opposites. These patterns of tubal pulsation establish self-identity by generating the feelings that we recognize as ourselves. They give a dimension to existence by creating an inside and an outside, a depth and a surface. This inwardness and outwardness are central in the anatomy of feelings and self-concept.

There is a basic thought-feeling process to all perception. This is to expand, swell, reach out and then pull back, shrink, contract. We go toward the world and then return to ourselves in a never-ending cycle. It becomes apparent that stress and distress disturb these patterns of pulsations. Sometimes there is a conflict between two poles: we reach out and shrink at the same time. We over-extend and lack the ability to pull back. Or we shrink and lack the ability to expand. Under these conditions our cells begin to lose their range of pulsation, and feeling, thinking, and acting as well as our self-identity is affected.

Cells reach out to the world, cells move away from the world. They take in and let out. How the cell expands and contracts is a statement of assertion. How it maintains pressure is a statement of self-perception. How it takes and gives is communication. The cell creates internal pressure to ward off external compression. This pressure continuum generates self-identity.

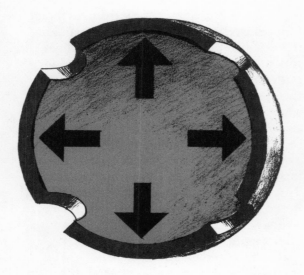

IMAGE ONE. A cell with its interior asserting pressure toward the outside. The notches depict passageways to and from the world.

IMAGE TWO. Pressure coming from the outside is resisted by a thickening of the cell wall.

IMAGE THREE. In the interchange between the world and the self there is a continuing exchange of pressure and a shifting thickness to the cell wall.

I   EXPANSION, SWELLING, MOVING OUT

2   CONTRACTION, SHRINKING, MOVING BACK IN

3   THE CONTINUUM OF ON-GOING EXPANSION AND CONTRACTION

Gravity exerts a pressure of 15 pounds per square inch which we have to resist. We have to be sensitive to the pressure created by the world or ourselves. With too much pressure we get compact and dense; with too little pressure we swell up from the inside like a blowfish removed from water. If the pressure builds up from inside out or outside in gradually, the membranes thicken. If pressure on the outside wall is insufficient, we expand into the environment. If membranes are weak, they leak out or simply explode. If pressure is quick and sudden the membranes get rigid like steel bars. This continuing recognition of pressure and accommodation to it must remain constant if we are to maintain an identity. As the cell consistently or abruptly alters its anatomy, it also alters its identity.

IMAGE FOUR. The cell is an entire universe, a miniscule planet, a complex ball, a source of incredible organization. Nothing is left to chance. There is the outer cell membrane; the inner nucleus, the container for the chromosomal material; and the energy sources —ATP, DNA, the mitochondria. Most importantly, the cell contains, in modified form, everything that a multi-celled gigantic organism does. It has a recognizable structure, an outside, an inside, central specific organs, and a network of tubes and tunnels for the circulation of fluids. There is layer upon layer of organization. Substances travel specific routes for delivery and transformation. Pressure is transmitted through a series of regulatory plates intensifying and diminishing. The notches on the surface indicate exits and entrances. A cell and its tubal passageways give the whole feeling of an inside as well as a surface. The force can be regulated by the layers that control and generate pressure.

One cell develops into cells. Separateness is an illusion. A circle becomes a colony, a ball of cells, and then an organization which elongates into a tube with empty and thick compartments. Tubes swell to become pouches.

4 CELLULAR ARCHITECTURE: LAYERS AND TUBES

IMAGE FIVE. A collection of cells makes a ball. Two layers become three through cell migration. This ball begins to structure space into hollows, pouches, a central core. This space intensifies cellular pulsation.

IMAGE SIX. Now there are three layers— outer, inner, middle. The middle layer gives rise to muscle, while the outer layer gives rise to skin and nerves, and the inner layer becomes the organs. The formation of a tube will begin from the elongation of the inner layer.

5 THE LAYERING OF INNER SPACE

6 THE BIRTH OF POUCHES AND DIAPHRAGMS

IMAGE SEVEN. One cell becomes two through polarization. This division takes place through the formation of a tube or tunnel—two pouches connected by a passageway. Each pouch has a nucleus. As the inner substance migrates to the two pouches, a sphincter is formed and a closing-off or division is made. The pattern is clear: elongation and separation. From an expanded tube a pouch forms, then swells, and finally closes off to make two from one.

IMAGE EIGHT. At an early embryological stage a tube forms inside a sphere, the beginnings of the nervous system and the head.

7 THE ANATOMY OF SEPARATION: PROJECTION AND INTROJECTION

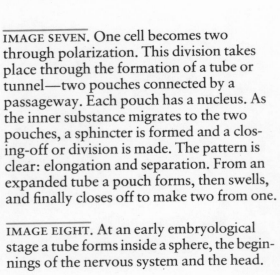

8 THE DEVELOPMENT OF A TUBE

IMAGE NINE. The cell has generated tubes and hollows, layers of insides. These begin to elongate and to pouch. These tubes are the blood vessels, the intestines, the spinal cord and skin.

IMAGE TEN. The layers of the human are manifest—an outer tube of skin and nerves, a middle layer of muscles and cartilage, and an inner space for the organs of nutrition and respiration.

9 THE ORGANIZATION OF MULTIPLE TUBES

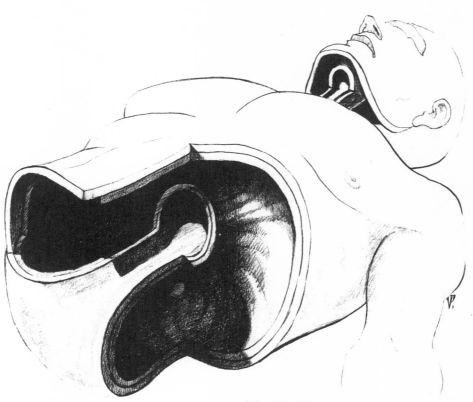

10 AN INSIDE VIEW: THE CONTINUITY OF SPACE, LAYERS, AND TUBES

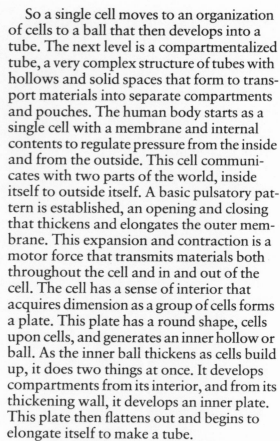

So a single cell moves to an organization of cells to a ball that then develops into a tube. The next level is a compartmentalized tube, a very complex structure of tubes with hollows and solid spaces that form to transport materials into separate compartments and pouches. The human body starts as a single cell with a membrane and internal contents to regulate pressure from the inside and from the outside. This cell communicates with two parts of the world, inside itself to outside itself. A basic pulsatory pattern is established, an opening and closing that thickens and elongates the outer membrane. This expansion and contraction is a motor force that transmits materials both throughout the cell and in and out of the cell. The cell has a sense of interior that acquires dimension as a group of cells forms a plate. This plate has a round shape, cells upon cells, and generates an inner hollow or ball. As the inner ball thickens as cells build up, it does two things at once. It develops compartments from its interior, and from its thickening wall, it develops an inner plate. This plate then flattens out and begins to elongate itself to make a tube.

Inside this compartment emerge the basic passageways—an internal tube for the transportation of food substances, an outer tube which makes boundaries and divisions, and a middle tube which makes muscles.

These further develop into a highly organized ball and a compartmentalized structure of tubes, pouches, hollows, and connecting membranes. One end of this process develops an inside, and the other end an outside. A series of insides and outsides become an anus and a mouth, a brain and spinal cord. Thus the ball has become a tube with at least three layers—an inside, an outside, and a middle. The outer layer of skin and nerves, the ectoderm, is for communication. The middle layer of muscles and blood vessels, the mesoderm, provides support and locomotion. The inner layer of organs and viscera, the endoderm, provides nutrition and basic energy. The inside is in contact with the outside through the mediating mesodermal level. The outside is the boundary, the social self. The inside is the secret, deep, ancient past and present. The middle is the volitional self, modulating between inner and outer. The inner tube transmits materials from place to place over long distances and through the layers from surface to depth. The generalized function of the three layers—ectoderm, mesoderm, and endoderm—is associated with three specialized pouches, the head, chest, and abdomen.

Early cell proliferation, going from two to four, from four to eight to sixteen to twenty- four on up, keeps the surfaces in direct contact with each other. Cells touch one another. This direct contact clearly demonstrates the principle of tissue connectivity. In early embryological development all tissues and organs are intimately connected; the heart and the brain are just two surfaces apart. The heart beat is tattooed right on the brain. No nerves are necessary. As development continues there remain vestiges of remembered contact. This is information, an intimate knowing. We are linked by the connectedness of all our tissues. We are a sheet of cells, twisted, bent, curved, rolled into organ systems and tubes and then into an organism. Deep layers, remote areas are affected by contact at a distance.

The internal connection of all layers gives rise to tissue consciousness, the sum of sensations from all levels of cells in a pattern of trillions of surfaces and internal environments. This gives birth to individual self-awareness.

12 THE GENERATION OF TUBES AND LAYERS

the pulsating pump

Pulsation is the in and out of all life and begins at the cellular level. The pumping action of a cell is essential both to transport itself and its contents, and for the exchange of nutrients. Many cell pumps join together to make larger and larger pumps. This pumping action will become the basis for many other functions—liquid exchange, breathing, movements of food intake, and excretion.

The whole organism is, then, a series of peristaltic tubes, pulsating with different intensities and amplitudes. The spine, muscles, stomach, heart, and brain all move at different rates of expansion and contraction. The nerve centers of the brain, as well as certain hormones, regulate rhythmic peristaltic waves, making them faster or slower. When scared, we are a fast-pumping peristalsis. When aroused, we have fuller pumping. When we are sad, the pumping function quivers. If we are depressed our peristalsis is dampened. Stress and distress lead to a breakdown of both tubular structure and peristalsis.

Pulsation is highly flexible and capable of adaptation to forces. The pumping action maintains the pressure that inhibits the atmosphere by sustaining the membrane itself and permitting the selective entrance and exit of substances.

A flexible tube is an ideal structure to oppose gravity and to organize uprightness. Organized horizontally, it allows for vertical swelling and shortening, and then lengthening against gravity, like the tube of a plant that builds a bark structure. Being erect is a pulsating process. The anti-gravitational muscles work through a pattern of shifting pulsation to sustain uprightness. Uprightness requires the ability to tolerate pressure as well as generate pressure. Conception and growth for the human occur first in the most optimal situation, the womb where there is little gravity. Then the embryonic liquid self and the womb establish a tubal connection that regulates fluid pressures.

Flexible tubes contribute to the maturation as well as the birth of our feeling. Soft tissue has a feeling state of tenderness and vulnerability. Rigid tissue has the feeling state of being capable of attack or penetration.

The wide variety of human postures is evidence of individuals' unique accommodation to the gravitational struggle. Developmental struggles and their concomitant emotional structures are visible in tubal weakness and spasticity. Swollen cavities often indicate pressure disturbances in feeling and in function, for example, emphysema and asthma. Compressed abdomens can cause reproductive and elimination problems. Pressure on the neural system from within or without creates nervous problems from headaches to loss of muscular control. Feeling and posture, our very self, is a function of pulsation. It is this process that gives rise to our thoughts and image. These facts have enormous implications for psychological understanding.

We, as self-reflecting creatures, take in, hold, and give back what was taken. We use and transform the world. We are also embedded in a bigger world. Reality in its deepest sense is the organization of all of life shaping itself. We, then, as the soul of life, are this pressure pump connecting all the layers of existence in the known and unknown worlds—from the atom to the cell, from the cell to the macrocosm of the universe.

Wave movements occur continuously in pulsating tides called peristalsis. They evolve as the basic expansion and contraction of a cell—a reflection of the currents of cytoplasmic inter-cellular movement. We are a series of peristaltic longitudinal and vertical waves.

The first vertical wave involves nutrition and respiration, the internal layer of the tubes. To assist this wave there are pumping stations—the vaults of the head, the pelvis, the diaphragm of the torso, the hard palate, the tongue, the glottis, the larynx, the pelvic diaphragm as well as the skull and the feet. The next wave connects the nervous system, the internal and external senses, and transports information in and out, up and down. The basic peristaltic waves of the neural tube flow from cranium to cauda equina, from brain to visceral ganglia, to the great outlets in the limbs and skin. In the neural tube the fast waves of the central nervous system and the slower waves of the automatic nervous system are found. The next great wave is the support and locomotion of the bones and muscles. Waves of muscle tone support the upright position. The long slow waves of the red muscle fibers close to the spine and the anti-gravitational muscles maintain verticality without effort, while the shorter, more eruptive waves of the white fibers give gestures of immediate response. These slow and fast patterns of muscle tonus are transmitted to the outer world as aggression and softness. They exit at the hands, feet, genitals, mouth, eyes, and body wall. The deepest waves are the hormones. They are tied to the blood waves, but have a real cyclical outpouring. There are fast hormonal waves of neural transmitters and the epinephrine energizers; there are slow waves of thyroid and the pituitary growth hormones.

The building of a structure for these waves can be seen in the liquid movement of slugs and worms. In worms the horizontal head-to-tail waves are interspersed by periodic rings of constriction. These appear sausage-like and function like a pump. These rings act as valves to build compression and make separations and compartments.

The outside of the human body reveals the head, chest, and pelvic swellings with constrictions at the neck and waist. Internal anatomy shows that the vertical waves must transverse more valves. In the swelling of the head there are rings at the palate, sphenoid bone, and foramen magnum separating the skull into those structures above and below it. The lower valves in the head include the palate, tongue, glottis, vocal cords, and hyoid bone as well as the muscles around the nape of the neck, the trapezius and scalenes. The next valve is the throat which divides the torso into two parts, head and chest. The major internal valve is the diaphragm separating the chest from the abdomen. The pelvic floor acts as the lower end to anchor the sacrum and pubic bones. Finally, the feet in interaction with the earth form the last valve.

Pulsatory waves are horizontal as well as vertical, from head to toe. They also have a circumferential flow, like circular rings at right angles to the horizontal flow. This right angle flow of pressure on the horizontal and vertical flows creates the pressure for standing, for specific human awareness and functioning. This transverse wave is intensified by the valves so that a powerful series of forces is transported.

The interaction of the waves, compartments, and diaphragms develops the pressure that resists gravity. All play an important role in uprightness. The transverse waves as well as the peristaltic action of the tubes act as a force against gravity. Two waves interact—one to push down, one to push up. The feet in conjunction with the ground form a reverberating drum.

Rings or tubes that become weak or spastic can affect the wave function—how we stand, move, emote. Stiff, rigid tubes or rings constrict the waves and speed them up. Weak or swollen membranes dampen the waves and slow them down.

EXPANSION
SWELLING

CONTRACTION
SHRINKING

CONTINUOUS
EXPANSION
AND CONTRACTION

13   THE EXCITATORY AND PULSATORY
CONTINUUM

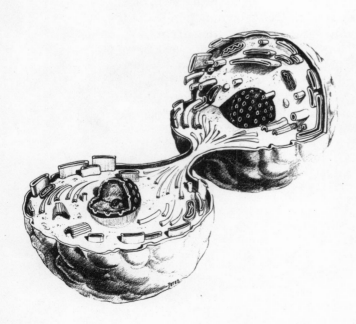

IMAGE THIRTEEN. The organization of basic pulsation and its relationship to the generation and maintenance of excitation. The swelling-shrinking, expanding-contracting function of the cells, with its ion interchanges, establishes a continuum of in and out, an accordion or pump-like action. This pump-like pulsation helps maintain the excitatory interchange, the polarization phenomenon that changes the shape of the membrane. The action of the pump creates an outer ring or limit where expansion ceases because of outer pressure (Image 1) and an inner ring where pressure and density limit compression (Image 2). There is pressure in two directions, outward and inward (Image 3). This movement circulates environmental substances from outside in and vice versa. It also circulates internal substances through channels within the cell and between cells. Note the ports or exits and entrances. You observe an inside, an outside, and a middle as well as a dynamic morphology, a continuum of changing shapes. Pulsation emerges.

IMAGE FOURTEEN. The contents of the cell polarize and project. These projections are pseudopods, contents moving from inside out. Reversed movement, from outside in, means the introjection of substances. These introjections and projections reflect the pulsation continuum. Continual pumping is a pattern of motility that supports these basic expressions and establishes a moving form.

The changing shape of the heart is an example of how pumping action sustains electrical circulation. The heart takes blood in, holds it, then expels it. It has a changing form for its identity. It contains only so much fluid, then expels it. The inner and outer rings are the limits for itself and they represent the hollow space that transforms the liquids into other liquids to be expelled.

14 PRIMARY POUCHING AND PASSAGEWAYS

IMAGES FIFTEEN, SIXTEEN, SEVENTEEN. Early embryological images of pouching and layering, their development and function. A colony of cells with an inside and an outside makes a chamber. This chamber is a swelling, a pouch, with squeezed space or sphincters at either end. The squeezings or sphincters serve as exits and entrances as well as pressure regulators. This pouch together with its sphincters creates a pumping action.

From this pouched tube will develop the various compartments—head, chest, abdomen-pelvis. At the pelvic end, that area where end products are transformed, the genitals, anus, bladder and legs develop. At the other end will form the mouth and entrance for the major senses as well as the breathing tube. In the middle will begin pouches of transformation and inner circulation—the heart, abdomen, viscera. Rings of separation between the pouches develop into diaphragms, separators, sphincters. Contact with the outer world is one of exchange and exits; the contact with the inner world is generation of excitation; and the middle world sustains excitation. A pump, then, is an interaction among the wave patterns of the three layers, the diaphragms and sphincters, and the wave patterns of the three pouches.

The various energy passageways and the currents of pulsation are early forms of assertion, to the world and away from the world. We move to the world to project, we come together to introject.

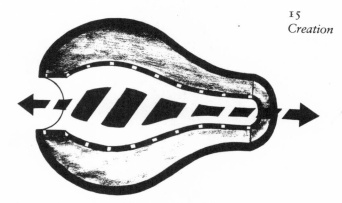

15 THE LAYERED PUMP

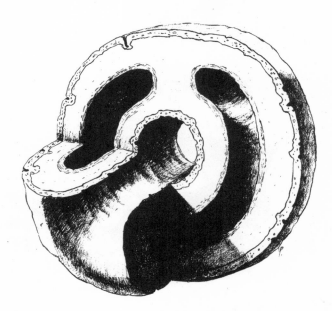

16 A CROSS SECTION OF TUBAL LAYERS

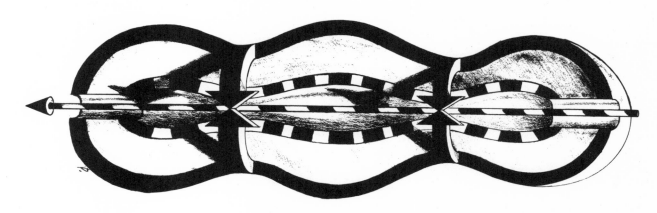

17 THE MULTIPOUCHED TUBE: FROM PULSATION TO PERISTALSIS

IMAGE EIGHTEEN. Evolution from a cell to
a colony, to an organism organized as dif-
ferentiated tubes and pouches, capable of
moving itself in the world. The pouches of
the head, chest, abdomen, and pelvis; the
rings of the neck, waist, mouth, and anus are
fully developed. The organism now can
creep, crawl, reach, take in, push away.

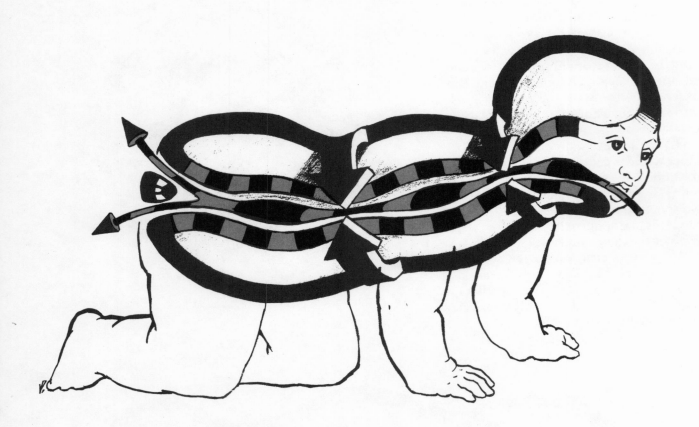

18 SELF-PROPELLING PERISTALSIS

IMAGE NINETEEN. Uprightness. Uprightness is the ability to structure and coordinate tubes, layers, and pouches in the field of gravity. Image 17 is the precursor of uprightness, Image 18, the first steps towards it, and Image 19, the completed structure.

The erect human form is based on heredity, the intensity of inner pulsation, the channeling of excitation, and human need. As the child grows, the center of gravity moves from the head and chest to the pelvis. This permits uprightness. Uprightness is actually a powerful combination of various layers of excitation interacting with various pouches. The most powerful flow of excitation occurs in the inner tubes, seen in the dotted lines, where there are strong rhythms of breathing, oxygenation, digestion, nutrition. The middle layer moves and supports excitation. It serves as containers and chambers. It is action oriented and not as freely motile. The outer layer of flexible skin and nerves is least motile.

Pulsation is a function that produces basic feelings such as joy, goodness, vitality, and excitation. Since there is a serial organization to the build up and transmissions of our insides, sensation and motility are transmitted from one pouch to another. For pulsation to travel throughout the body in waves from head to foot, there must be clear organization—within each pouch and between each pouch and the next. There should be a feeling of excitation from inside out and outside in. Continual patterns of emotional distress, however, may cause tubes, layers, and pouches to become rigid and elongated, dense and compressed, swollen and stuffed, or collapsed and weak. The pouches may telescope into each other so that the neck shortens, the waist disappears, the chest collapses, the head or belly swells. Under these conditions the tissue no longer supports waves of pulsation; thinking, feeling, action and uprightness are affected.

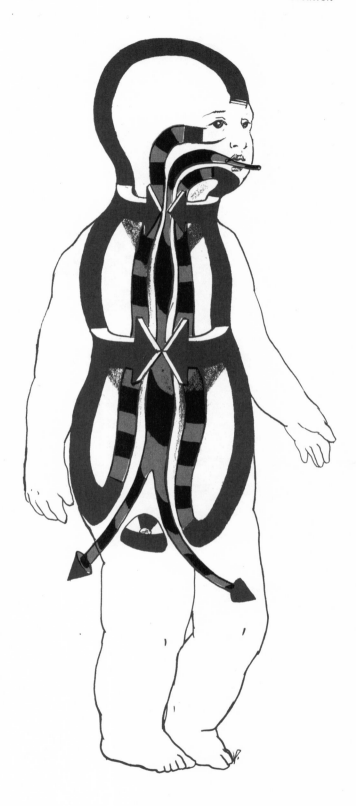

19 PERISTALSIS AND UPRIGHTNESS

20 THE EVOLUTION OF PERISTALTIC LIFE:
FROM ANIMAL PULSATION TO HUMAN
MOTILITY TO UPRIGHTNESS

from motility to movement

Patterns of motility and patterns of action and movement are different. Movement describes how creatures get from place to place. From the perspective of somatic process, movement is mechanical. Joints and bones bend, fold, turn, glide; muscles lift, pull, push, squeeze, contract, elongate. Motility, on the other hand, rises from the metabolic processes of existence. The cell's excitability, its expansion and polarization are examples of motility. Emotional arousal such as anger or fear is another example.

Animal life is mobile and motile. There is elongation, a stretching, and its reciprocal, contraction. This basic rhythm is seen in all living animals, grossly in the heart, and microscopically in cells. It has a rotational torque or twist. The movement of life is like a corkscrew, a twisting elongation and a twisting contractive return, a rubber band effect. This twisting, pulsating, stretching, shrinking serves two purposes: it is a miniature pump circulating nutrients, and it is also a means of propulsion.

There are three patterns which take us from animal motility to human movement, uprightness, and walking. They are reaching out, pulling in, and pushing away. They resemble swimming movements in that their combined interaction establishes propulsion.

These patterns begin in the womb where the fetus floats. To assist in its own birthing, the fetus elongates and compresses, generating twists and turns. In the womb, floating, twisting, and turning help to pump liquids. This torquing generates a powerful force to facilitate birth.

After birth an infant continues to elongate, stretching and rotating limbs and torso. He seeks the breast, explores space, and rolls over. The child gradually masters the use of the hands, arms, feet, and legs and coordinates this new mastery into creeping and crawling. These early stages of locomotion resemble horizontal swimming—reaching out, pulling back, pushing away.

Learning to stand upright involves further mastery of another succession of movements, from creeping to crawling, to squatting with the arms extended, to pulling up, to standing, and then, finally, standing alone. All of these movements involve combinations of reaching out, pulling back, and pushing away. Horizontal swimming found in creeping and crawling becomes upright swimming in squatting, standing, and walking.

Standing is not a mechanical event, bones resting upon bones supporting weight on the earth. Nor is it achieved through tonus of anti-gravitational muscle. Standing is a vertical pulsatory pattern, a pumping action. It is a rhythmical pattern of expansion and contraction that moves excitatory fluids through space. In standing we learn to sustain the pressures that make for an effective human pump.

Walking is a swimming movement—reaching out, pulling back, pushing away, but done vertically. The whole organism elongates, torques, rotates, flexes, and contracts. Walking requires the rotation of the spine, the pelvis, the shoulders and head; it further requires that we stretch the limbs out and pull them back.

IMAGE TWENTY-ONE. The basic swimming movements viewed from standing. Their interaction, development, and mastery take the human organism from the embryo to uprightness, from creeping to walking. These swimming movements in their many developmental stages reflect the continuum from motility to movement.

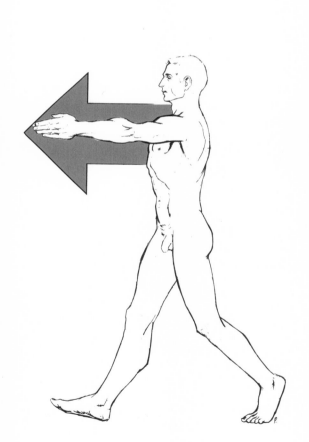 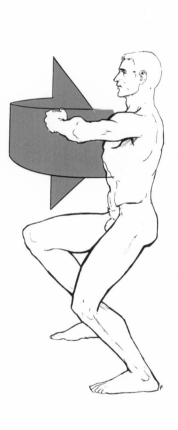 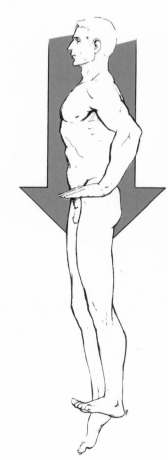

21 THE BASIC SWIMMING MOTIONS: TO REACH OUT, TO PULL IN, TO PUSH AWAY

The human being has many layers: skin, fascia, muscle, bone, organs, liquids. The skin stretches and contracts in a continual pattern. The skeletal muscles change shape in a symphony of adjustments to maintain uprightness. The bones shrink and stretch with varying pressures. Organs are a dynamic wave of peristalsis waxing and waning. The liquids of the body are propelled by the flexibility of organismic pumps. We swim in the current of an environment we create. We extend, then come together, then extend again. This is what motility is about. Motility is expansion and contraction, elongating and shortening, stretching and gathering. It is an inner flow that is different from movement. Movement refers to skeletal muscle, to action that has to be available for stop and go functions. The striations of skeletal muscle permit inhibition and movement that is capable of interruption yet is able to brace and shift tone or direction.

IMAGE TWENTY-TWO. In utero the skeletal muscular system is quiet. The blood system, cardiovascular system, and internal organs are motile. The organism is free floating. Pulsation is dominant. The embryo expands and contracts, elongates and shrinks with internal vegetative movements. The inner contents are active, the walls supportive and containing yet still.

Later, embryonic swimming occurs. Tides of pushing, elongating, and resting build up the internal pressure and energy that become kinetic in internal swimming and, later, at birth, in pushing out. Motility, at its peak, is the baby trying to swim out of the womb in a giant turning pattern. Legs extend, arms squeeze down and push away, the head inches forward. The random kicks in utero are part of an expansion-contraction pattern which extends into internal swimming, a birth-movement, and acts as a precursor for the complicated patterns of movement to come.

22 FLOATING

IMAGE TWENTY-THREE. Creeping is an extension and development of the basic swimming motions. It involves extending the spine with one arm and one leg while flexing the neck. At the same time the alternate leg slids, pushes, pulls, holds, contains. It is a balance. Push away from the surface—pull toward the surface—incorporate the new surface. The infant extends himself as one end pushes away and the other end pulls him. The skeletal muscles now begin to be active in channeling the basic internal tube actions. Muscle-brain connections begin to happen.

23 CREEPING

IMAGE TWENTY-FOUR. Crawling depends upon previous organizations: birth, sucking, creeping. Rotation involves pressure build-up, extension, and the use of the weight of the pelvic pouch or head to turn, elongate, and generate pressure. Crawling involves mastery of arms and legs—pushing up, balancing, and moving forward. As the brain grows, the infant rehearses or practices the organization necessary for being erect—using the head, eyes, mouth, hands, face, limbs, torso. While creeping is basically motile activity, crawling is the conscious use of the skeletal muscles.

Crawling increases independence. The beginning of language accompanies crawling, a further tool in overcoming helplessness. Crawling also frees the head for scanning, encouraging an organization of space that leads to sitting. It makes pulling one's self up possible. The child practices stiffening his legs and increasingly demands parental help to master the use of voluntary muscles. Pulsation begins to change and the tides of motility give rise to kinetic movements. Crawling brings closer the mammalian functions of crouch-walking, falling, the use of the arms for balancing and the steadiness needed in early walking.

24 CRAWLING

IMAGE TWENTY-FIVE. Humans organize the world from the head-up position in which the front of the body is exposed to the environment. Movement is now up and down as well as forward and back. From this position, the senses of the face, the sense receptors for pressure and temperature receive a great increase in stimuli. With soft parts more exposed, human knowledge of the world increases. At the same time new defense postures are necessary, flexing the muscles of the chest and abdomen. Standing involves stiffening the legs and spine to achieve erectness, the use of the arms for propulsion, the balance of weight from foot to foot, and the rotation of hips and shoulders around the spine. Thus, to stand the legs push off and the arms pull forward to reach to the world. Standing involves vertical mastery of the swimming movements. The child pulls and pushes through a gaseous environment.

In this further transition from motility into movement, there is a dialogue between spontaneity and control. Inner reflex is gradually replaced by outer levels of control. If mechanical volitional movement dominates activity, action becomes robot-like with little inner experience. If volitional systems are poorly integrated, controlled movement is affected. Impulses dominate.

This progression from floating motility to voluntary interaction contains the feelings of fear, joy, frustration, goal accomplishment, playfulness, contact. Psychological and emotional birth parallels motor development, our growing sense of "I," a sense of assertion, the knowledge of how we organize ourselves to translate pulsatory peristalsis into voluntary action. This is the drama.

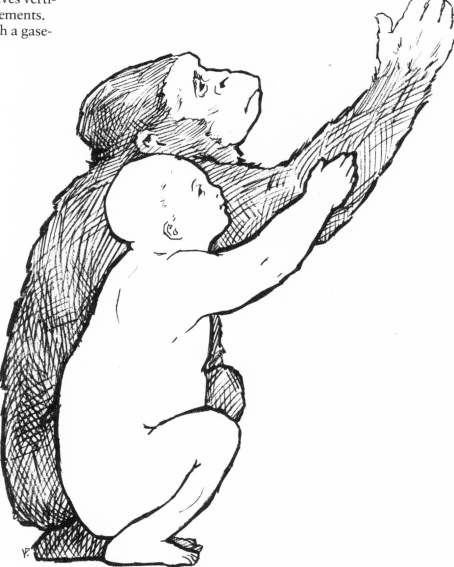

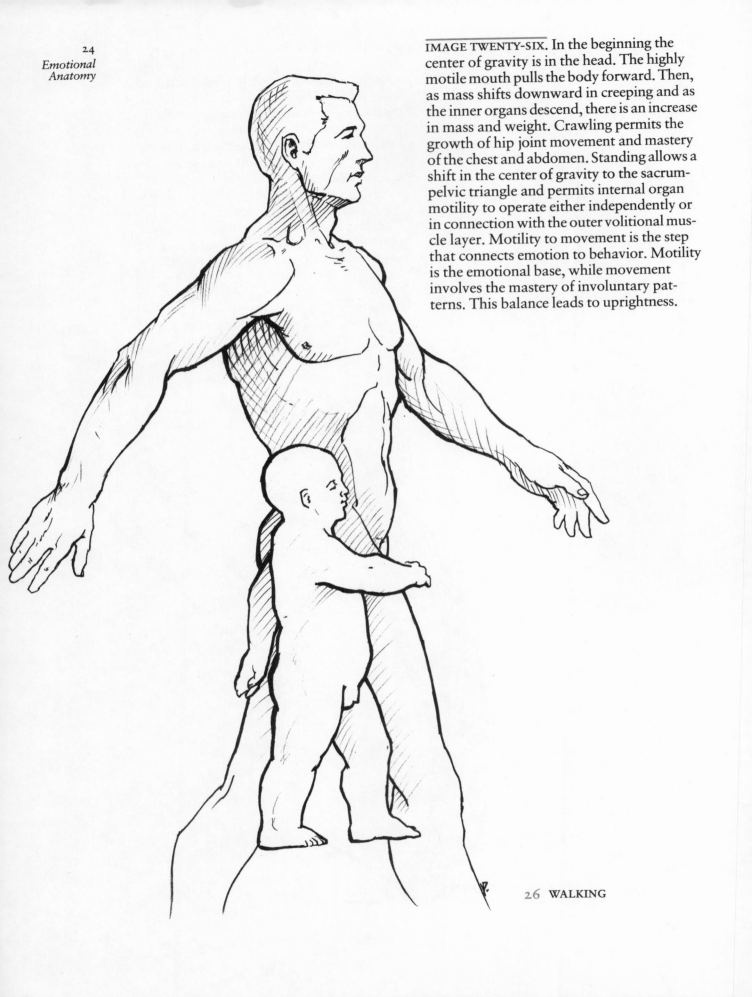

IMAGE TWENTY-SIX. In the beginning the center of gravity is in the head. The highly motile mouth pulls the body forward. Then, as mass shifts downward in creeping and as the inner organs descend, there is an increase in mass and weight. Crawling permits the growth of hip joint movement and mastery of the chest and abdomen. Standing allows a shift in the center of gravity to the sacrum-pelvic triangle and permits internal organ motility to operate either independently or in connection with the outer volitional muscle layer. Motility to movement is the step that connects emotion to behavior. Motility is the emotional base, while movement involves the mastery of involuntary patterns. This balance leads to uprightness.

26 WALKING

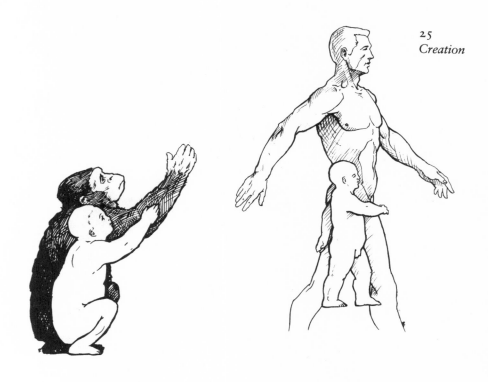

**27 FROM INSTINCT TO VOLITION: THE
LAYERING OF CONSCIOUSNESS**

two

the body plan

GROWTH OCCURS according to a general organizing principle. It is not a haphazard process. This organizing principle involves a body plan that establishes a shape genetically, personally, and societally. The body plan is revealed in the way we grow embryologically. A circumferential cell evolves into a tube that organizes itself vertically and horizontally with an inside and an outside; a ball becomes a series of layers and compartments. These compartments swell to become pouches—the oral, thoracic, and abdominal-pelvic cavities. This multi-layered pouched tube stretches, shrinks, pulsates, and begins to fill itself in.

This compartmentalization and layering from which organs grow is central to the organizing plan of the body. Tubes interrelate to establish pumps which move the materials of life and maintain the motility of existence. Pulsation acts as a moving membrane, swelling and shrinking, to create three walls—an outer wall, an inner wall, and then a middle one between these two worlds. The plan of the body, in its simplest form, is to construct spaces and structures to maintain pulsation so that specialized activity can occur.

The outer body wall contacts the environment. This outer layer or tube has to do with information, protection, and the setting up of a boundary between inner and outer worlds. It is intimately related to the central nervous system, a neural layer that compartmentalizes, separates, divides, and communicates. The outer layer is called the ectomorphic layer. The middle or mesomorphic layer contains the muscular-supportive structure—muscle, bone, cartilage, tendons. This middle layer provides support for the outer and inner tubes. The deepest layer is the endomorphic layer, including the inner body wall, and the cavities and organ systems of digestion, assimilation, and respiration. These are the functional layers of the body. These three layers are like envelopes —neural, muscular, and organ—bound together by the liquids of the body. There is, in addition, a hormonal layer or network, consisting of those liquids that generate and regulate how we are aroused, how we reproduce ourselves, how we transmit information, feeling, substances. This deepest layer of all is the invisible flood of hormones in which complex fluids maintain or encourage specific behaviors. The body plan, therefore, actually consists of four layers, three visible and one invisible.

These tubes and layers have varying degrees of pulsation and varying degrees of flexibility. They relate to each other and give rise to certain experiences. The neural layer gives rise to the language of touch, sensation, sound, external senses, temperature. This layer thinks in terms of light and surface contact, pictures, and movement. The muscular layer thinks in terms of stretching, pressure, compression, and rhythm. The inner layer of organs thinks in terms of liquidity and motility, waves of contraction and expansion. The hormonal layer thinks in terms of various excitatory qualities and arousal, fires which roar or are dampened.

Human structure as tubes and pouches, layers and compartments, walls and spaces creates a pump-like function: the pump of the muscles and bone, the pump of the internal viscera, and the neural-hormonal pump. The pumping action generates the pressure that organizes body spaces to maintain their structural integrity. This pressure also reflects an internal state and generates the feelings that we recognize as ourselves.

Somatic process is concerned with how patterns of good feeling, patterns of stress

and distress, and patterns of emotion are organized as particular kinds of pulsation. In the beginning of life, in utero, there is a powerful pulsatory pattern set up between the mother and the embryo. This pattern supports the flow of blood through the umbilical cord and then begins to fill out and support the life of the embryo as the embryo lays down tubes to channel the fluids that are exchanged between it and the mother. Pulsation is how spaces are created and sustained; it is a basic kinetic morphology that generates form.

Motility has to be appreciated from the inside; it is the vitality of the pulsatory pattern, the power and intensity of organ pulsations that give energy and personal identity. True identity does not arise sensorily, from muscle movement patterns or the approval of others, but rather it arises from the quality of sensation from the internal pulsatory waves of the smooth muscles of organs. Feeling and sensation that arise from the inside tell us "this is who I am." Self-image is based upon patterns of sensation from the interior; it is the geometry of these sensations that arise from our process, hungers that are acted on by the nervous system and the skeletal-muscular system, that bring rewards. We know ourselves from the inside out.

In the inner spaces of the cranium, chest, abdomen, pelvis and where liquids accumulate and move, in the uterus, bladder, the kidney, and the brain, the most profound functions of life are found. Offspring grow, water purifies, food transforms, blood electrifies, sensations of motility become patterns of thought. When these spaces lose their functional integrity, qualities of digestion, sensation, and thought change. Just as a tumor compresses and displaces its surrounding tissue and disturbs normal functioning, so when internal spaces become dense or collapse or endure pressure, there is a change in the quality of sensation and pulsation that make up self-identity. The result is fatigue and an inability to maintain a human shape, a shape of caring in connection to the world.

Internal metabolism is a way of thinking. A way of thinking precedes words; it is a process that is transmitted by genetic tradition. A single cell, in a certain way, is a brain. It pulsates, expands and inhibits, and reflects about the nature of resistance it meets on the outside and the kind of pressures it has to generate on the inside. Regulation of pressure by the cell sets the limits of its expansion and contraction, of how it constructs the inner world to meet the outer world. In this way the cell thinks about its own shape, and how the world presents itself. Much pressure, little pressure. The cell generates sensations and reponds, it gives itself out to the world. If there is a conflict between internal pressure and external pressure—should the cell expand or should it contract?—a pause or synapse is created as in inhibition of action. This internal layering of the organism—hold it, wait, expand—is a form of memory. It is organismic thinking.

IMAGE TWENTY-EIGHT. The organization and development of tubes and hollows. The organization of a hollow starts in the embryonic ball, organizing a dimension in space that has not existed before. Outer, middle, and inner tubes form and develop. Hollows develop into pouches with accompanying passageways. The body plan of tubes, layers, and pouches is revealed.

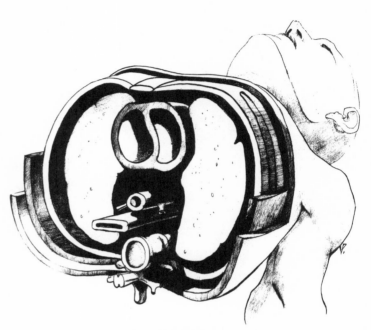

THE LAYERED HUMAN TUBE

THREE TUBES

THREE LAYERED POUCH

IMAGE TWENTY-NINE. A cross section view of the development of tubes and layers. There is a dense structure, a space, and another elastic membrane. Embryological development transforms these three layers into the complex human form: the outer body wall, the aorta, the heart, the lungs, the spine, the muscular layer. All aid in expansion and contraction. Imagine pressuring this tube inwardly and outwardly—too much outward pressure and it swells, losing its boundary; too much inward pressure and it gets compact; too little pressure and it collapses.

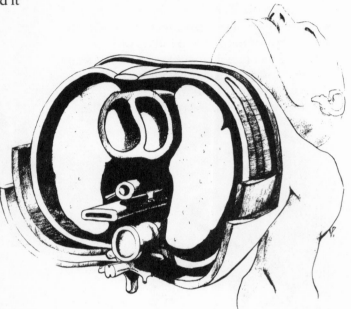

29 THE LAYERED HUMAN TUBE

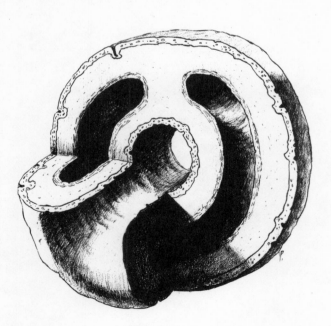

IMAGE THIRTY. Tubes as elongated channels with a central space for nutrition
and respiration, a middle layer for support,
and an outer layer for communication and
information.

31
The Body Plan

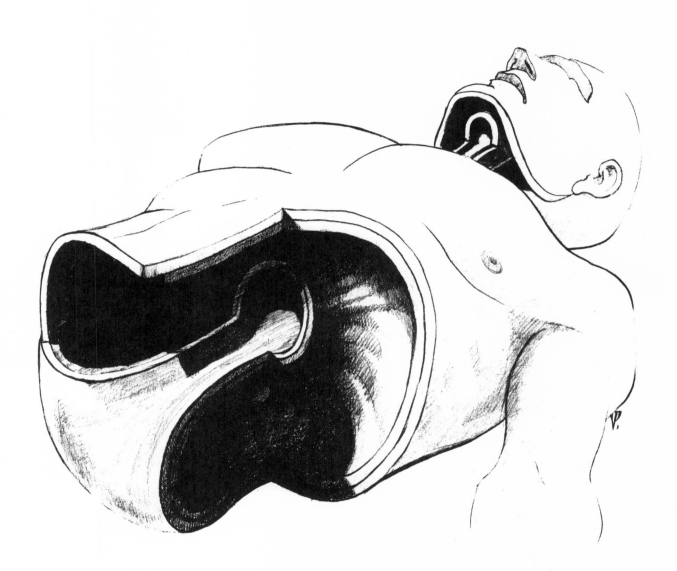

30 THE BODY PLAN: THE STRUCTURES AND
SPACES THAT MAINTAIN PULSATION

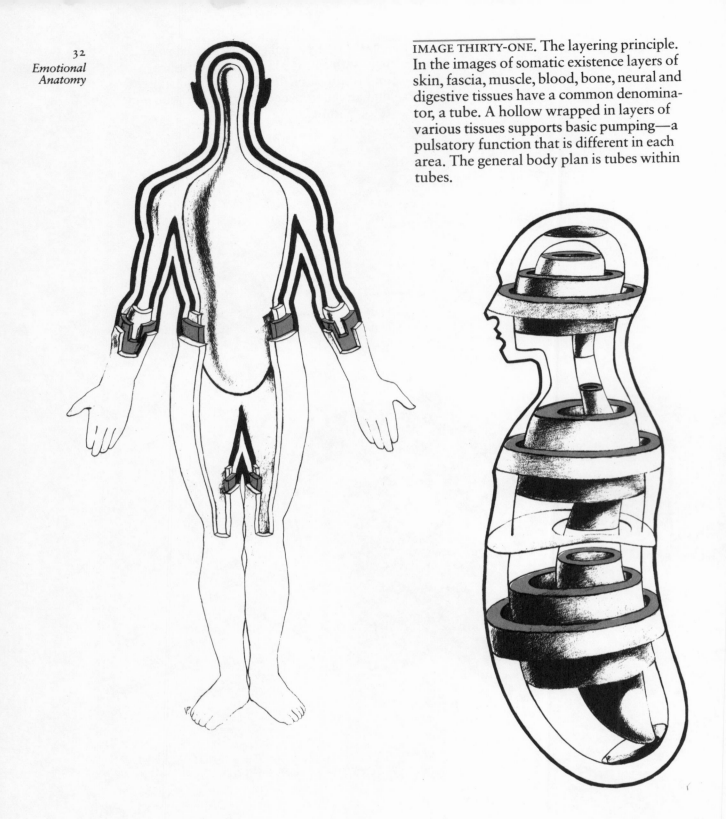

IMAGE THIRTY-ONE. The layering principle. In the images of somatic existence layers of skin, fascia, muscle, blood, bone, neural and digestive tissues have a common denominator, a tube. A hollow wrapped in layers of various tissues supports basic pumping—a pulsatory function that is different in each area. The general body plan is tubes within tubes.

31 TUBES: LAYERING AND THE PUMPING FUNCTION

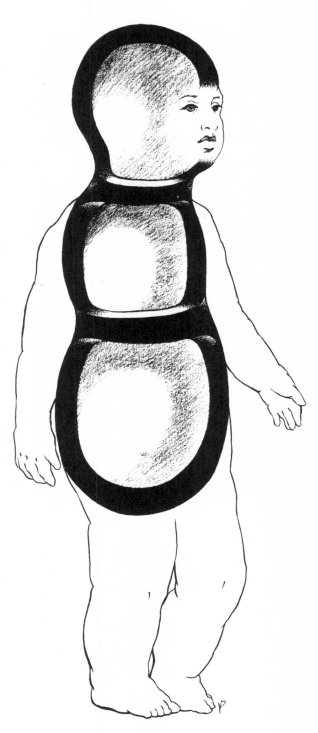

IMAGE THIRTY-TWO. Compartments or pouches for specialized functions. The organs are specific locations of generalized functions. The heart pumps blood but is a specialization of a total body function. The brain extends to the entire organism by means of the spinal and nerve systems. The digestive system involves not only the stomach but the entire system of internal organs.

In each of these pouches expansion and contraction are at work, producing a pump-like function. The patterns of this pulsation differ by pouch. The pumping of the brain differs from the pumping of the heart; the pumping of the intestines is different from the pumping of the muscles. So the general body plan is pouches, layers, and tubes with a mouth or intake end, an exit end, and a middle for processing—all functioning as a pump.

32 VERTICAL PUMPING: COMPARTMENTS
AND SPHINCTERS

IMAGE THIRTY-THREE. The interaction of all components of the body plan creates an accordion-like effect. The pouches, in conjunction with the various diaphragms, neck, thorax, cranium and pelvic floor, help regulate pressure, head to toe, side to side. The accordion function maintains segmental and longitudinal pulsation.

IMAGE THIRTY-FOUR. Pulsation—the true force supporting verticality. The human being stands erect because he is a vertical concertina, a motile accordion.

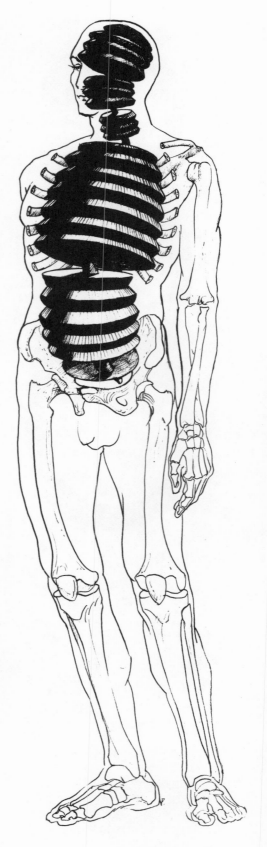

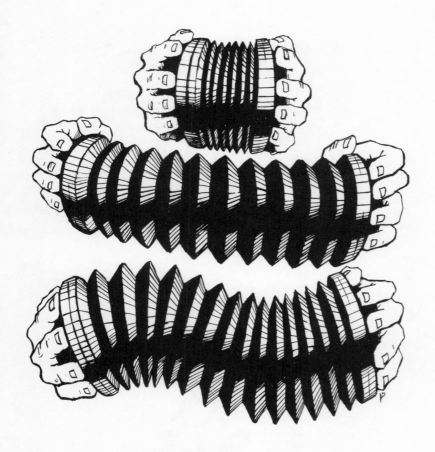

33 THE ACCORDION

34 THE ACCORDION MAN

Muscles and their connection to movement are easily observed under the skin. They respond immediately to experience. We feel tight or tense in readiness for action, or we experience different fluttering patterns in the heart as fear or joy. Muscles give immediate contact with reality, externally through patterns of skeletal action and internally through the increase or decrease of the heart rate and activity of the digestive system.

The mark of living organisms is their ability to respond. A general property of protoplasm is contractibility accompanied by excitability. This provides an effective motor force. Muscle cells specialize in contraction and elongation. Groups of cells form elongated packages that are then bunched or bundled. By increasing in length and depth, they acquire powerful forcefulness for pulling, pushing, sustained compression, rhythmical continuous activity, or for long, slow, wave-like action.

Since muscle is connected to every layer of the brain and spinal cord, conceptually, the brain and muscle could be viewed as one organ. In this sense muscles are fat nerves. This muscle-brain link is man's executive organ for social and personal development. It is part of a continuum serving the organismic need for survival, social and individual action. This chapter, while describing anatomy, also directly speaks about psychological analogies, the blueprint of our brains. Muscles serve the function of movement. In the occipital section of the brain and its section for movement, the cerebellum, patterns of action are recognized. They are judged to be friendly or not through the emotions of the mid-brain or learnings associated with the cortex.

What are muscles? They are the first part of the general process of organismic life, sustaining postural shape, executing action, supplying information about self-identity and boundaries. Muscles provide the capacity for social roles and gestures. In short, they are important since they represent a general function—to ensure movement either of the total structure or of internal substances.

There are three types of muscle, two which are related to structure and one which is not. The two are skeletal striated muscle and cardiac striated muscle, and the other is smooth non-striated or organ muscle. Skeletal or voluntary muscles are associated with volition, yet this can be misleading. These muscles drape the skeleton. They cover and cling to it like a suit of clothing at both the deep and superficial layers. The muscle layering includes the fibers of the small muscles of the skeleton that regulate posture, and the anti-gravity muscles, including the inter-axial muscles such as the inter-thoracic, and the exo-axial, such as the limbs and those that link the limbs and back to the spine. These groups can, for the most part, be controlled. At the same time they are deeply anchored in programmed reflexes. An example is the flexion contraction of fear. These striated muscles are specialized for fast action but they can also function at faster or slower rates.

Skeletal striated muscle has pale fast fibers and red slow fibers with extra hemoglobin. The fast fibers are for rapid action such as immediate response or the quick patterns of the startle reflex that provoke attention. The slow fibers are necessary for postural and social stances that provide a sense of stability and reliability. The slow and fast responders are only part of a continuum. There are also intermediate fibers. Many times there is conflict between the fast responses and the slower responses. Layers of muscle contraction war with each other and herein lies a basic conflict for the personality. The deeper levels generally resist change. They represent the homeostatic mechanism. Deep or slow muscle patterns represent our stable self. Change in this arena requires a form of reparenting. Emotional relearning is not to be confused with muscle relaxation for the fast acting group.

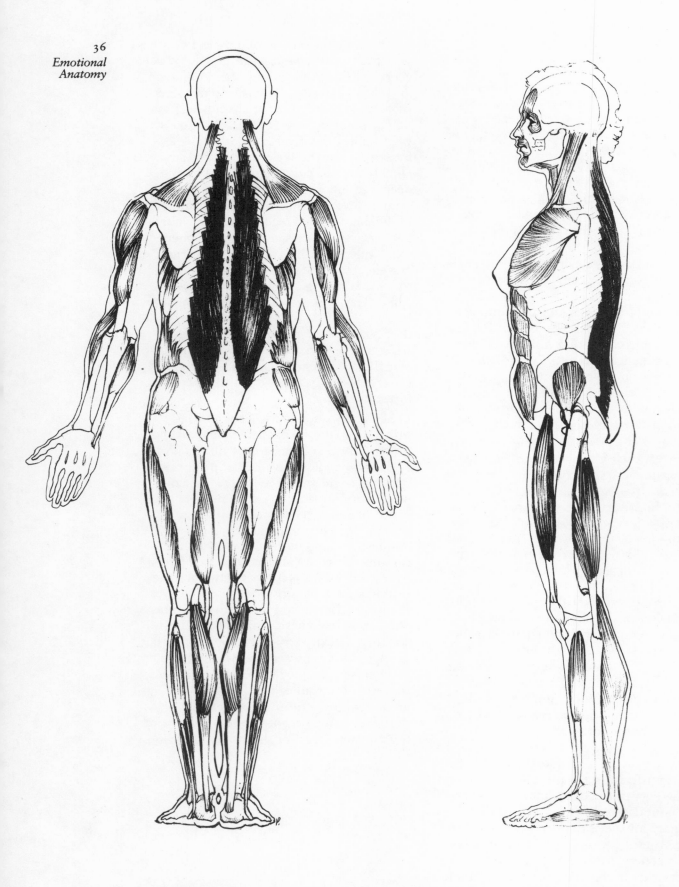

35 SKELETAL MUSCLE PUMP: BACK VIEW   36 SKELETAL MUSCLE PUMP: SIDE VIEW

IMAGES THIRTY-FIVE AND THIRTY-SIX show the surface and deep muscle layers. Cardiac muscle represents an internal dominion because the heart and the major blood vessels lie deep in the thorax and head, yet have branches on the surface. Cardiac muscle is striated, meaning it has a series of cross bridges. These bridges connect heart cells so there is no interruption of electrical currents. The heart muscles are like a friendly social network. They seek to spread and facilitate the flow of excitatory currents and maintain a rhythm of self-regulation. The heart is influenced by the autonomic nerves which suggest rates of speed for contraction and even amplitude in response to many conditions, especially emotional states. It should be self-evident that the cardiovascular tree with its huge central station pictured in IMAGE THIRTY-SEVEN is actually a gigantic pump, an expansive, contractile, receiving, expelling pump.

Smooth muscle is influenced by the autonomic nerves but is poorly organized for sophisticated pulsation. What it does well is make a prolonged, slow, sustained wave like the heart expelling blood or the skeletal muscle shortening to do work. These long and slow waves are seen in all visceral tissue, blood vessels, hormonal ducts, intestines, urogenital tubes. A steady wave of contraction is needed for moving things along a tube or expelling them. The best examples are seen in the esophagus or the womb.

Skeletal muscle illustrates how muscle tissue is effective in its continuum of elasticity. Skeletal muscle ends in collagen, heavy fascia, tendon, and bone. Each is successively less elastic. Thus there is a decrease in the rate of give and the acceptance of pressure. This permits a controlled rate of contraction over a tissue bridge that ranges from highly elastic to less elastic. Force is transmitted from high motility to low motility. In smooth and cardiac muscle, force is transmitted against itself and against what is incorporated, blood or food. Thus compression is limited by content.

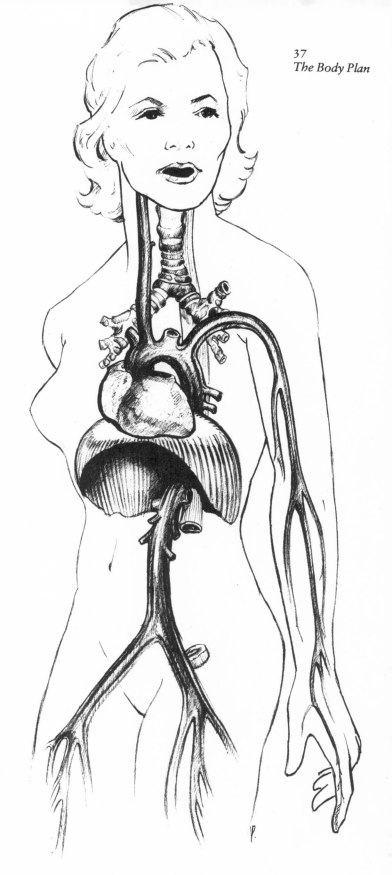

37 THE INVOLUNTARY MUSCLE TUBE:
CARDIAC AND BRONCHIAL MUSCLES

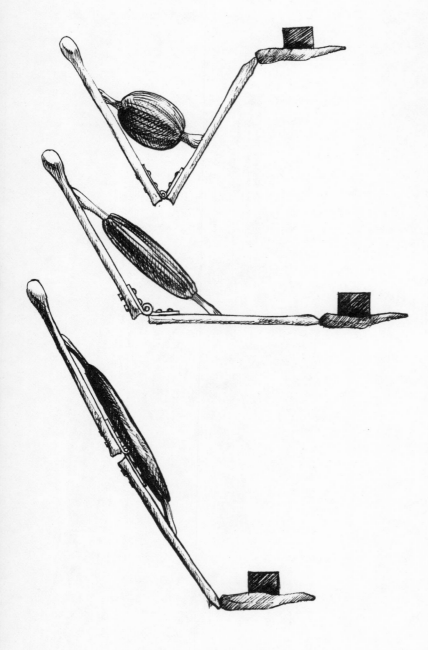

This categorization of muscle type and function emphasizes the pumping action of muscle. Throughout the book this action is referred to as the accordion. The opening and closing of muscles is a continuum of expansion and contraction from more to less. In expansion and contraction there is no maybe but only how many fiber bundles are involved. This expansion-contraction is a pump with many variations. How the muscle pump functions is depicted in IMAGE THIRTY-EIGHT. The muscle extends and contracts, a hydraulic function that generates pressure by shortening. Shortening requires lengthening. Thus the muscles that shorten in turn elongate the opposite member. The bicep extends up to a point and then the stretch reflex comes into play, shortening and reversing the process. This is an antagonistic response, somewhat like a pully system in which one side shortens and the other lengthens. Through these movements pressure is generated, contained, and dissipated. We can reach out, pull in, hold tight.

The three muscle types invoke three pumping patterns: the continuous rhythmical waves of the cardiac pump, ceaseless, altering only in speed and amplitude; the long, sustained, contractile, slow-paced wave of smooth muscle, varying only in intensity and duration; and the two waves of skeletal muscle, the phasic, quick, limited action seen in the biceps or the long standing, steady, contractile action of the spinal column and anti-gravitational muscles. These different pumping actions, quick and sharp, sustained and smooth, rhythmical and insistent, create a continuous pulsation pattern. This pattern is a feeling that we recognize as our identity. We recognize ourselves in the waves of sensation that keep the flow of ourselves constant, in the rhythmical thump-thump-thump of the heart; the internal feeling of the intestines and lungs moving in and out; and the overall feeling of the body wall expanding and contracting.

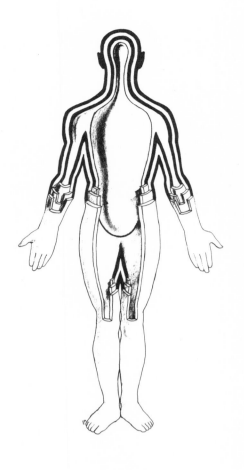

IMAGE THIRTY-NINE. Muscle layering and pump function demonstrate further that we are a tube-like structure, with an outer muscle layer offset by deeper layers of muscle. Image 39 shows this tube-like structure outlined in layers. To facilitate efficient pumping stations, the structure is segmented into head, chest, and abdomen and offset by the diaphragms of the neck, waist, etc. As a wave goes through the organism there is compression longitudinally as well as circumferentially. There is an elongation and compression and a rhythmicity that narrows, expands, and supports pressure as needed.

Muscles give the sense of containing and controlling ourselves as well as others. When muscles and their pump function are rigid with fear, dense in defiance, swollen in false pride, or collapsed from lack of support our self-mastery is weakened, our self-esteem is diminished and our mastery of the world is affected.

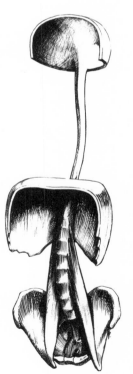

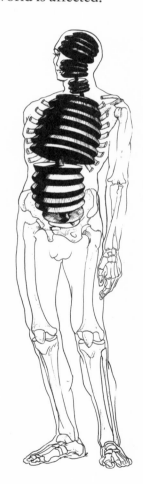

39 GENERALIZED AND SPECIFIC PUMPING

bones

Bones give support and substance. Bones are living tubes, inner honeycombs sheathed by dense, compact cells. With this arrangement the body is able to withstand tremendous pressure, compression, and tension. Bones have a rich nerve supply on their surface, and thus, can feel pain. Bones transmit weight and give rise to a sense of inner strength. All muscles attach to and move bones. The skeletal frame gives the tubes support yet is moveable so we are not just robots stuck in space. In order to build a body image through the proprioceptive nerves, the bones must move in their sockets and joints. This gives an appreciation of the transmission of weight from segment to segment and is the basis of the ability to take pressure.

Bones play another role. They offer protection for the delicate structures that keep intact the prehistoric ocean where the blood cells oxygenate and the white cells offer immunity and self-recognition. These cells are born, incubate, and grow within the inner labyrinth of bone. When mature they replace the old warriors and workers, or multiply as needed to repel invasion.

A mother gives support to her children because their young bones have not hardened enough. If, as children, we do not get this support from our parents we try to gain it by using contracted muscles for the support of bone. Failing that, we feel collapsed and lack an inner feeling of reliability. Severe muscle contraction will distort bones just as severe lack of muscle tone can strip away the supportive function.

Bones are also living pumps. They are dense and compact networks of tubes that give form and feeling. IMAGE FORTY displays the function that bones serve.

Bones do not lie in direct contact with each other but are connected by joints. Bone joint surfaces have a liquid and semi-liquid interior, IMAGE FORTY-ONE. This permits a space that makes up a pump. Expansion and contraction create spatial changes in these spaces. This pumping helps circulate spinal and other tissue fluids and forms a continuum of tissue with many levels of pressure, fast to slow moving. The osseus pump carries weight, controls speed and motion, and gives rise to sensations of compression and inner cohesiveness.

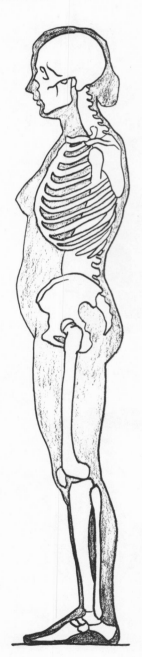

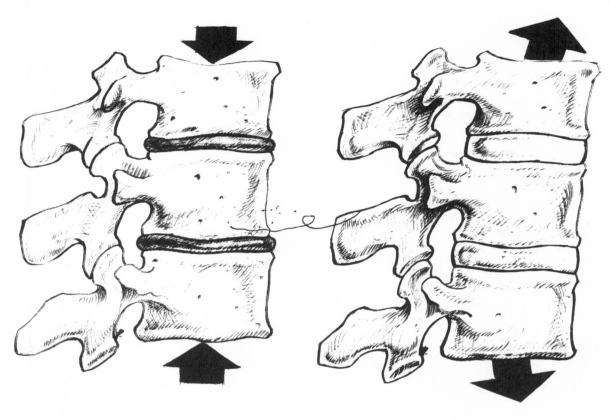

Overstiff and weak bones are portrayed in IMAGE FORTY-TWO. Bones can increase their ability to receive pressure and weight, and thus transfer the support function from muscles and organs, back to bones, cartilage, and tendons. This increases the feeling of density and safety of the inward structure.

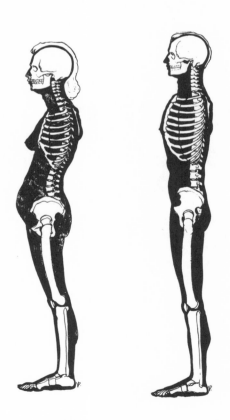

42 BONES: COLLAPSED AND RIGID

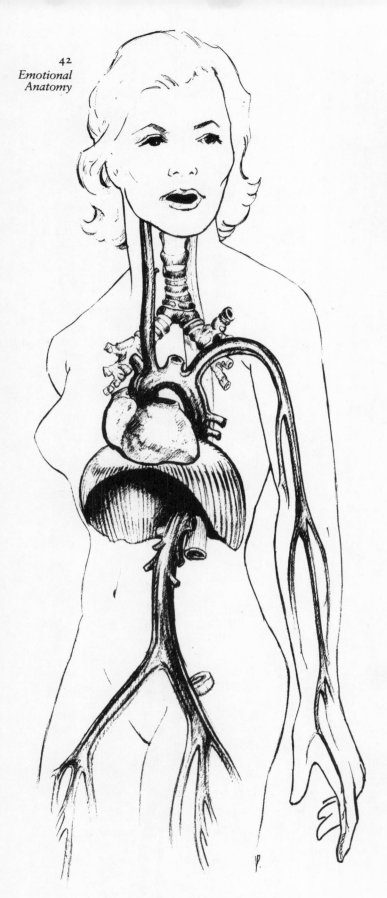

When there is injury to or disease of the joint, like arthritis, the spaces are altered or obliterated. This can also happen in long-standing repressed rage or frozen fear. Rigidities compact the organism, eliminating the spaces of the pump. Sensations of elongation, reaching, and contraction are lost. This diminished sensation affects body image as well as feelings of moving with confidence. Frozen or weak structures have problems feeling inner motility or support; their loss of bone integrity leads to feelings of inner fragmentation. Parents who do not hold their children or give enough early containment may force them to rigidify their muscles in order to gain a sense of support. If, as adults, these people try to relax their muscular contractions they will experience anxiety because they lack feelings of inner support from their bones and joints.

the blood tree

Blood is an electrified fluid that is given tidal thrust by the heart and its vessels. Blood circulation is a generalized function with a specialized local organ, the heart. Blood and gas exchange takes place all over the body, yet the heart is the central pump.

The heart and its main branch, the aorta, send energized fluids through the body. The aorta, accompanied by the esophagus and the vagus nerve, pierces the diaphragm. Here the intimate relationship between the heart and the dome of the diaphragm is established; breathing and the heartbeat communicate directly. The location of the vagus nerve also makes clear that breathing and heartbeat give rise to sensations that flood the whole organism.

IMAGE FORTY-THREE. The relationship of the heart to the rest of the organism and the muscular pumping function. Rigidity or weakness of the skeletal muscle wall can affect the functioning of the heart and lungs, and give rise to feelings of anxiety and inadequacy. Inhibitions in taking in or expelling set up rigidities in various parts of the blood tree, causing a multiplicity of mechanical and emotional problems.

breathing

Respiration means to respirit, to animate. Breathing is the visible experience of a continuous action we make to remain connected to the planet. Breathing is a specialized form of pulsation. The continuum of in and out constitute the rhythms of respirations. When we work faster or are enraged or fleeing we breathe more. When we are awake and standing our breathing uses more of the chest. Respiration and awakeness thus go together. When we are asleep we breathe more slowly. When we lie down we are more like animals; we become belly-breathers.

The continuum of inhalation and exhalation is like a wave. The breath increases in amplitude, rises to a crest, and then gently wanes. We inspire, the wave emerges and peaks, then we gently expire, pause, and inhale again. If we are excited the wave increases in pitch. When we are relaxed, we breathe deeply into the belly. When life demands we breathe vigorously, we recruit more of ourselves by extending our breath into the abdomen, neck, and head.

Respiration is a pulsation with several rhythms: fast, slow, deep, shallow. The core of breathing is the diaphragm with its lower abdominal chamber and its upper thoracic and cranial vaults. The sweep of the respiratory muscles keeps the flow of gases and pressure constant. As infants we respire in the upper body, belly, chest, and head. As we grow, the pelvis becomes more involved; we coordinate breathing with creeping, crawling, and standing.

Breathing is, most importantly, a basic pulsation that reveals somatic and emotional activity. Breathing is a pump with a total organismic expansion and contraction of 18–22 cycles per minute. Breathing goes from head to toe as a pervasive and constant activity. It can be compared to the pattern of the heart as a total spiral contraction, unwinding, filling; a separate but synchronized filling and emptying of the upper and lower chambers. Just as arhythmic heartbeats set up poor circulation, so can incomplete respiration give rise to feelings of suffocation, defeat, helplessness, and fear. Since the heartbeat and breathing are interconnected, they influence one another. When the heart fails for lack of energy, then breathing has to work harder to make up the difference. When respiration is fatigued, the heart has to work harder.

The function of respiration is to capture, transport, and expel gases. To do this a tube between the inner body and the environment is established; at the same time there is a tubal connection within the body. This tubal architecture develops from the micro tubules of intercellular life into the umbilical system and then, finally, to the mature respiratory system. The entire body is a tube that pulsates with waves of expansion and contractions in respiration. If this tube is not flexible with a wide spectrum of motility we are limited in terms of both the action we can pursue and the feelings we allow to emerge. The richness of our thought and imagination is affected. If muscles do not receive sufficient blood or oxygen, we cannot act. If the brain suffers a lack of oxygen, we become comotose, dull, inattentive. If, on the other hand, too much oxygen gets to the brain, as occurs in anxiety states, we feel impelled to act. So tubal pulsation and respiration are more than anatomical acts, they are states of mind.

In summary, the movement of respiration reflects the powerful archetypal patterns that have roots in the tidal action and basic pulsation of the cells. This basic pulsation is seen in all living tissue at all times.

the anatomy of respiration

Respiration is the pumping and channeling of fluids as gases and vapors. Breathing as pumping is affected by the tubal structure. Embryologically, breathing arises from the endodermal tube, where energy function is paramount and where food has to be oxidated to supply the fuel for intense growth. The digestive tube and the respiration tube emerge from the same homeland and are forever linked in the anatomy of the head, mouth, thorax, and abdomen. The mouth and nose share the head vault. Common tubes divide to become the trachea and esophagus, the highways to the lungs and stomach.

The respiration-digestion pump, with its tubes in the lungs and intestines, is aided in sucking in and expelling out by the contractile muscles of the mouth, tongue, esophagus, trachea, alvioli, and diaphragm. The air passageways share a common space with the organs of the head, chest, and abdomen. Increased muscle spasticities or weaknesses, conditions of rigidity, denseness, swollenness, or collapse, immediately disturb both breathing and eating. This occurs whether the constriction is in the mouth, neck, chest, or abdomen.

IMAGE FORTY-FOUR. Breathing is sucking in, pulling in, making a space, holding for assimilation and exchange, then propelling out. It involves increasing and decreasing thoracic pressure. Taking a breath is close to sucking, yet exhalation is not as passive as one might imagine. To expel it is necessary to use the muscles of the abdomen and the rib cage. The diaphragm ascends, the chest narrows, the lungs compress, and the air is expelled. Image 44 shows the excursion of the thoracic muscles of breathing as well as the cranial and pelvic poles. It involves the entire body wall. Breathing involves inhalation and exhalation; it is a bellows-like function.

Respiration involves both an external exchange of gases with the surface and an internal exchange of gases throughout the tissues. This is reflected in the basic rhythm of breathing—a four point event:

> Breath in
> Reach a peak—pause
> Exhale out
> Reach a valley—pause

The peak is rounded rather than sharp except in abnormal breathing situations where the pauses are prolonged and the peaks are jerky or escalated. This occurs in sobbing or gasping. The basic rhythm of 18–22 breaths per minute maintains a smooth pattern: in, wait for an exchange, out, wait for an exchange, O_2 hunger, in. This same pattern goes on inside us, deep at the cellular level, to fuel the fires of our existence; O_2 is pumped in and CO_2 is taken out at the cell membranes. So we breathe locally at the lung sac level and generally at the tissue level.

The heart and lungs serve to supply the messenger, blood, with oxygen and propulsion. The vagus nerve is linked to the heart, diaphragm, lungs and intestines and establishes a reciprocal relationship between the diaphragm and the pericardium of the heart. They beat together. The amplitude of the diaphragm affects the amplitude of the heart and vice versa. When we cry, the diaphragm hits the heart and the esophagus. Thus breathing, blood flow, and hunger are all intertwined. The tubes of disgestion and breathing give rise to sensations of hunger, emptiness, reaching out, taking in, filling up, expelling.

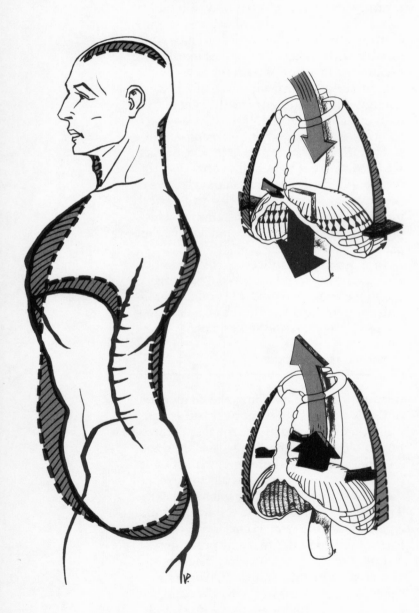

44 THE DYNAMICS OF INSPIRATION AND EXPIRATION

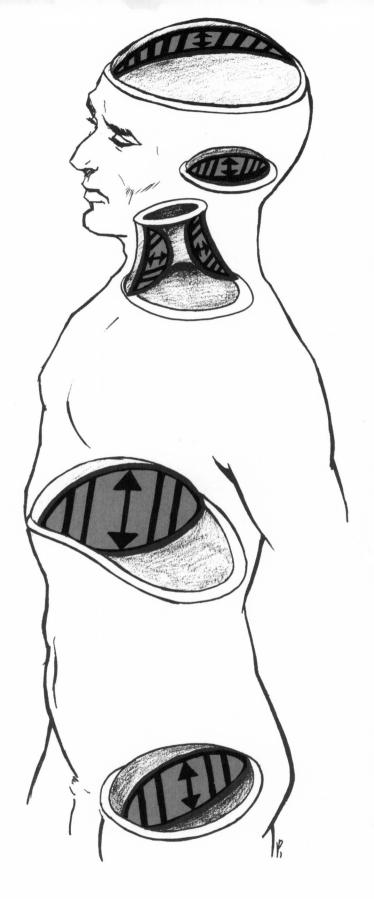

IMAGE FORTY-FIVE. Breathing is a form of extension and contraction—an elongation and swelling of the trunk and chest followed by a shortening or thickening of these compartments. Several diaphragms assist this process through enlarging the pressure flow and concentrating it. In the head pouch the cranial layering, dura, and bone serve as the first diaphragm. This brain diaphragm extends via the foramen magnum all the way to the sacrum via the spinal crural coat. Cranial pulsation has its own rhythm of 14 beats per minute set up by the ventricle and spinal fluids. The thick dural coat of the brain, along with the swelling of the brain stem, the protective sheath of the spinal cord, and the occipital muscles of the foramen magnum, forms the second diaphragm that regulates the internal pressure of the head. The tongue and sphenoid-ethmoid palate form the floor of the brain as well as the roof of the mouth and act as a third diaphragm along with the nasopharynx muscles, the glotus, the hyoid, sternohyoid, and omo hyoid bones, and the clavicle muscles. This diaphragm regulates the flow of pressure into the trachea pouch and, by controlling pressure from the lungs, aids in upright posture. Important blood, hormonal, and cranial nerves exist here.

The thoracic diaphragm consists of the chest wall or rib cage, the external and internal intercostal muscles, the inter-thoracic muscles and the two domes of the diaphragm. In this space the lungs and heart are enclosed as are the passageways or tubes of the esophagus, aorta, vagus nerve and vena cava vein. This fourth diaphragm separates the thorax from the abdomen. The abdominal-pelvic diaphragm is made up of the roof of the diaphragm, the lumbar spine, the ligaments, the psoas, the iliacus, and the floor of the pelvis. It is like a hammock made up of the bony pelvis and sacrum and their accompanying muscles. Inside this segment are found the organs of digestion, excretion, and sexuality. This fifth diaphragm serves to oppose the downward force of the inter-abdominal pressure that occurs with inhalation.

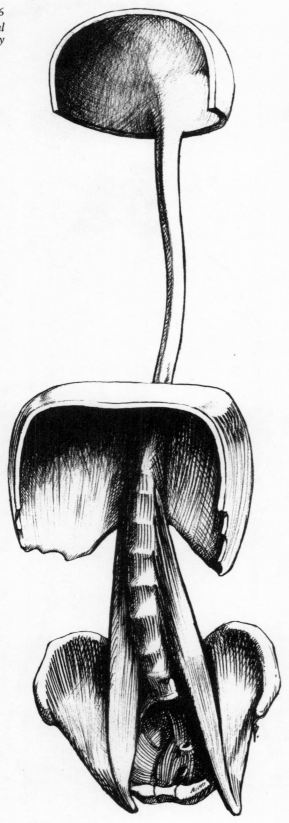

IMAGE FORTY-SIX. Externally, the human tube is composed of three bulges, the head, chest, and abdomen, and two rings, the neck and waist. Internally, leaves divide the tube in the middle and give it flexible ends. The middle leaf is the diaphragm with powerful piston actions that give rise to deep sensations of aliveness. The middle diaphragm also massages the heart and vagus nerve. It increases and decreases inter-thoracic and abdominal pressure. At the pelvic end sheaths of muscle support reciprocal movement. At the upper end the dural covering, the falx cerebelli and cerebri, and the spinal cord covering act as a flexible tube. This tube pumps cerebrospinal fluid. In addition, in the cranial pouch, the ethmoid and sphenoid bones together with the foramen magnum have the flexibility to ride up and down to increase or decrease pressure. The mouth and tongue also facilitate pulsation. In this way a complex series of internal and external valves operate to increase or decrease our breathing and its accompanying feeling of aliveness.

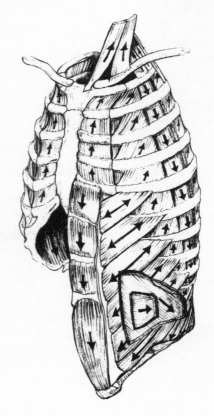

46 THE THREE MAJOR DIAPHRAGMS AND THEIR CONNECTIONS

47 THE MUSCLES OF RESPIRATION

IMAGE FORTY-SEVEN. The external muscles of breathing. The intercostal, the abdominal rectus and oblique muscles, and the transverse abdominal muscles, operate in unison in expiration and inspiration. Muscles of respiration and the chest are linked to the abdomen and neck. The movement of these muscles gives rise to the sensations that support feelings of power or weakness in oxygenation and physical activity. Rigidity of the neck, chest, or abdomen can lead to interference with the diaphragm. Spasm or weakness in the chest leads to difficulties in respiration.

IMAGE FORTY-EIGHT. Layering as a pressure regulator. Pressure tension permits the exchange of gases to occur and is essential for complete respiration. We know this pressure when we push on the chest, feel its decompression and then the recoil response. The layers and tubes of the body interact to create and regulate pressure. Tubes that are weakened do not support pressure but collapse, and experience fear and failure. Tubes that are rigid cannot expand and lead to eruptions.

IMAGE FORTY-NINE. The basic contractile property of tissue also makes respiration possible. Pulsatory peristalsis is aided by the action of the thoracic diaphragm. The interaction between the outer body wall and the respiratory diaphragm creates the pressure that maintains motility and supports human form. To control any action it is necessary to control both breathing and the diaphragm. To become still or silent the outer skeletal muscles must inhibit both pulsation and respiration. Internally, the diaphragm and the chest wall can be used to inhibit breathing.

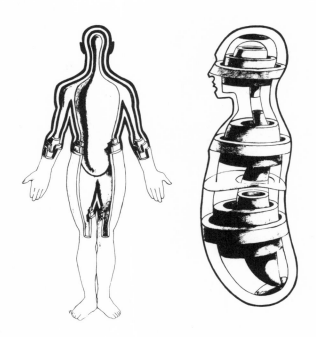

48 TUBES AND LAYERS: THE CONTINUATION OF RESPIRATION

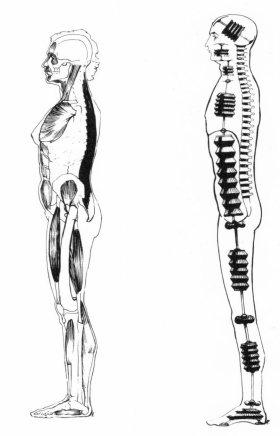

49 THE GENERALIZED AND LOCALIZED FUNCTION OF BREATHING

The tone of the tubes and the rhythms of respiration are controlled by the brain centers and the autonomic nerves. In the instinctual program of the autonomic system, the parasympathetic and sympathetic fibers in the diaphragm are similar to smooth muscle innervation in the intestines. There is a chain of regulation from the brain stem which integrates messages regarding gas content. The body is CO_2 conscious—if there is too much of it we breathe more; if there is too little we breathe less. The upper brain centers can override this mechanical program at will. The upper brain centers command: Hold still, count your breath, don't breathe, hold your breath, breathe more, breathe harder. These commands are sent via the phrenic nerves of the central nervous system that supply the diaphragm and affect its rate of pulsation and the spinal nerves that control the rib cage muscles. In this way the central nervous system gets involved.

The thoracic diaphragm consists of two muscles, the costals that attach to the ribs and sternum, and the crural muscle that attaches to the central tendon and the back wall of the abdomen, the quadratus muscles and lumbar spine. These two muscles receive nerve commands from the autonomic nervous system, the vagus, and the central nervous system via the phrenic nerves. So they are regulated both autonomically and voluntarily. Put another way, the voluntary muscles connect the cortex of the brain to the muscles of breathing.

Many techniques of meditation manipulate the voluntary control of the semi-voluntary process of breathing. In seeking to change consciousness, these techniques affect breathing by either depressing or inflaming CO_2. This produces high O_2 states which lead to hyperventilation, convulsive muscle action and an increase in sensations which dominate the attention centers. Or the CO_2 state is increased by depressed breath which leads to quiet hypo-oxygenation, a diminishment of drive, and then a trance state. These states activate or depress the heart and intestines. With O_2 increase, the body is inundated with sensation; with CO_2 increase, sensation is inhibited. The basic peristaltic wave becomes depressed or overactive; brain pulsations are lowered or increased, as in breathing. So meditative or breathing techniques indicate the connection between voluntary and autonomic control of breathing.

There is yet another process that overrides the autonomic regulation of respiration, and that is emotion. Fear, alarm, rage, and terror affect breathing. The cortical center stills the chest to control sobbing and the muscles of the mouth to suppress a scream. The chest clamps down to stifle fear and the diaphragm stops so there is no display of emotion. Alternately, it is possible to whip up the diaphragm to mimic rage or fear. Emotion can be so strong that we lose self-control; volition is overruled and sobbing or screaming begins. All these situations result in breathing patterns where the chest cannot move fully for fear of its own sensation or its own lack of control.

To control ourselves we must control our breathing. All three brain centers, the cortical-voluntary, the thalmic-emotional, and the brain stem-cerebellum represent the regulation of respiration. No breathing, no oxygenation. No oxygenation, no fire. No fire, no life. No life, no force. No force, no spirit. That is why the heart, brain, and breathing are so closely connected.

Respiration reflects the general function of expansion and contraction. To take in, contain, expel, to receive, transform, give back. To breathe fully is to have a range of swellings and shortenings. To fill the entire tube, the chest elongates, the belly swells and inhalation is experienced from the cranium to the pubic bone. To expire gently yet forcefully requires both thoracic and abdominal pressure, a soft rhythmicity that pulsates throughout the entire body wall.

If, however, tubes, layers, and pouches lack flexibility, then changes in expansion and contraction are reflected in breathing. Many breathing patterns display a narrow range of experience. Perhaps in early life a person was not touched very much or touched with hostility. In either case, a fear pattern dominates, rather than one of comfort or pleasure.

IMAGE FIFTY. A diaphragm that is rigid and a diaphragm dragging downward. Rigidity develops in the body wall as a brace against insults or disapproval. Weakness is a result either of having been served too well or of having assertions that received little response. In both cases the result is poor respiration and this affects how we work, respond, and love. Breathing becomes an effort that taxes or weakens us.

The entire organism, not just the diaphragm, is involved in respiration. The respiratory muscles need exercise to carry through their full range of motion. This involves all the muscles of breathing—the chest, abdomen, and skeletal muscle wall. Physical exertion, running, and exercise are useful as they increase general responsiveness and carry over to other activities in our lives. Yet these activities do not necessarily make lives more human or interactive. Full respiration is based on contact with others as well as with one's self.

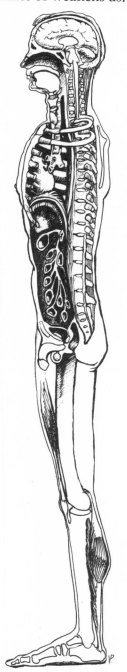

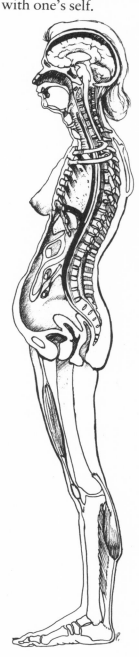

50 DISTURBED BREATHING: RIGID AND COLLAPSED

the brain and the nervous system

Excitability is the central component of the nervous system. Expansion and contraction are the primary actions in the muscles, whereas in neural tissue the primary actions are polarization and de-polarization. There are waves of electrical current in nerves and waves of actin myosin in muscle. Structurally the two are similar. Muscles are made up of elongated cells; nerves are made up of elongated axons. Muscles and nerves, strangely, have the same geometry. They are bundles of tube-like structures wrapped into bigger bundles and formed into even bigger ones.

Nerves start as cells with elongated bodies that connect at distant points. These neural tubes generate waves of excitatory impulses along their axis and transport protoplasmic fluids along their pathway. These elongated bodies are called tracts, nerves, or cords.

The nervous system originates in the neural tube of the embryo. It forms a series of bends and a series of pouches at one end. These pouches will later become the front brain cortex, the midbrain, and the hindbrain. From this neural tube, cell bodies send out axons, tubes, or nerves and the spinal cord is formed. Thus the neural tube consists of the brain, the spinal cord, and nerves that extend into the muscles and organs, establishing an intimate and direct link between the muscles and the brain.

The nervous system has two parts—the autonomic nervous system and the central nervous system. The autonomic nervous system is related to the viscera and basic life functions. Its home is the lateral part of the spinal cord and the medulla pons, also called the brain stem. The central nervous system resides in the forebrain, or cortex, where sense and muscle discrimination take place. Here is where planning, associations, and discrete actions are learned. It is the area of voluntary control.

IMAGE FIFTY-ONE. The nervous system is a tube within a tube, the neural tube inside the spinal column inside the body wall. The nervous system is a sort of chicken wire lattice. The central tube, the cord, has a dense structure that ends in a mushroom system at one end, and a root system at the other. It is a tube going down a central line, branching out, and forming a network. The nerves that attach to the organs and supply them are connected to the spinal cord in a structure that is somewhat like a spider web. If all the nerves were filled with a dense substance they would be stiff like tree roots and would graphically illustrate a network.

The nervous system network includes the dermal connective tissue structures with all their special sense receptors and the external skeletal muscles with their kinesthetic function of maintaining a connection to space and the outer environment. So the neural outside includes not only the skin and blood vessels but the voluntary muscles by means of the cerebrospinal system. The nervous system and brain connect the inside and the outside.

The nervous system, like all systems, is layered. These layers serve as protective channels and liquid conductors. At the same time the nervous system is a pump, pulsating, shrinking, and swelling, circulating spinal fluids, ventricle fluids, the fluids between nerves and muscles, and hormones.

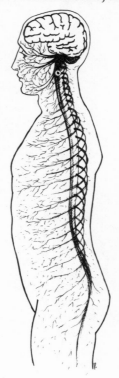

The nervous system regulates organ and muscle contraction as well as hormonal distribution, but in the case of hormones it is equally affected by them. In a certain sense the brain and nervous system are a hormonal gland. The nervous system has historically been considered to be some sort of electrical generator, since excitation and hormonal conduction are linked to it.

The nervous system is a tube which both generates and transports electrified fluids and hormonal and neural impulses. The pumping action of the system is directly related to the vitality of neural and neural-hormonal activity. For example, in cases of shock, endema or congealed liquid proteins create spinal cord stasis with a concomitant lessening of neural activity. With extreme cold there is neural inhibition and activity diminishes.

IMAGE FIFTY-TWO. The neural jellyfish. The nervous system is a hollow space, filled by fluids that facilitate the pulsation of the organs. The nerves are a central channel through which axon plasma is pumped. The pumping brain and spinal cord maintain a central liquid flow involving cerebrospinal fluid and the ventricle flow in the brain. The braincord system evokes the image of a giant jellyfish—elongating, swelling, emptying, filling. It maintains an internal electrified atmosphere that responds to action in the general cellular sea. This system is a part of the pulsatory pump of the whole organism, giving rise to electrical currents, excitatory patterns and hormonal fluids. These constitute the liquid motile anatomy that transforms micro behavior into macro behavior.

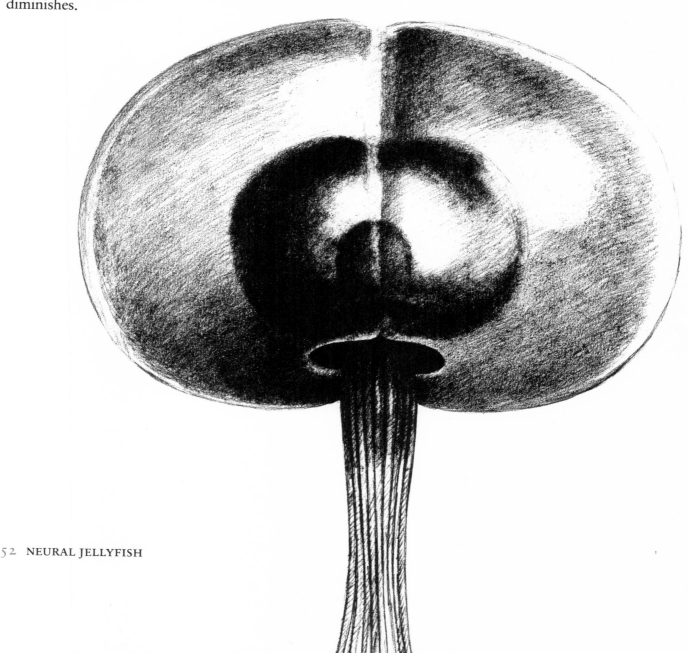

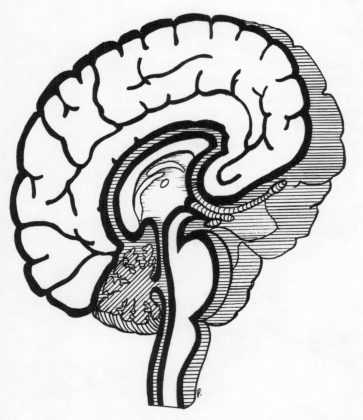

53 THE NEURAL PUMP: CORTEX, MIDBRAIN,
BRAINSTEM

IMAGE FIFTY-THREE. The outer, bean-shaped cortex, the fetal-shaped midbrain, and the reptilian-shaped brain stem. The three layers have a circulation network of fibers between them. The brain functions like a huge heart. It has four interior chambers called ventricles and a major exiting pipe, the spinal cord, which is like the aorta. Fluids are circulated to the whole organism through these pumping stations. The brain continuously pulsates at about 14–18 strokes per minute. The pulsatory systems of the various pouches in conjunction with the brain form one complete system.

The brain as a total unit pulsates. It also regulates the pulsation of the rest of the organism, which it is able to inhibit and intensify. As the neural system pulsates, the subjective phenomenon of streaming or vibration occurs, giving sensory self-experience as well as the deeper experience of neural wholeness. During fear or fight the organism reacts with increased pulsation of the intestines and heart, and the upper body becomes engorged, swelling and building up force to charge or run. Think of a jellyfish pumping faster to act as a battering ram, or pumping slower as in sleep.

Sometimes the brain wars with itself; one part is overactive, the other, underactive. The pulsatory patterns are irregular. The waves of rhythmicity have areas of diminished responsiveness similar to damaged heart muscle that upsets cardiac rhythms. The brain can inhibit or overactivate itself. Fear inhibits the brain. Rage makes it overactive. Terror and shock create inhibition and hibernation. Sadness shrinks the brain while anger disrupts and intensifies its rhythms. Defiance hardens the brain. Sexual arousal and love facilitate the rhythmic patterns, speed them up and intensify their amplitudes while overstimulation races and shortens the strokes. The brain, like the heart, is subject to fast and slow, normal and erratic rhythms.

Muscular tensions, spasticities, or weaknesses around the head and neck have a powerful negative effect on the brain and autonomic nervous system. Chronic muscular tension in the mouth and palate can interfere with the flow of brain pulsations, just as the shortening of muscle in the occipital atlas joints affects the circulation around the spinal cord. Muscular spasms affect the deep autonomic nerve regulators in the neck, affecting oxygen supply. Tension in the esophagus and lower pharynx can also affect the cranial nerves. Deep contractions of the neck muscle separating the head from the torso or spasms of the eye muscles or neck muscles stop the free pulsation of the brain. Pain and illness can be the result.

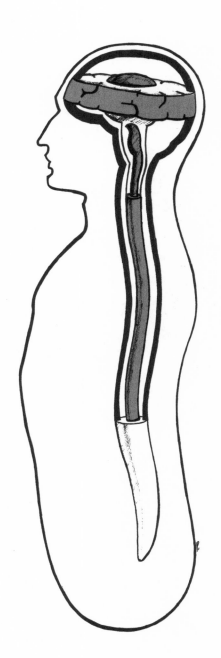

IMAGE FIFTY-FOUR. The three layers and tubal elongation of the nervous system. The outer ring of the cortex is richly supplied from the nerves and senses—visual, tactile, auditory, proprioceptive, kinesthetic. It is here that human time and space are determined. The middle layer is the thalamus where the emotional, time-oriented appetites live. Then there is the deepest layer, the cord, the serpent, the autonomic tube. In this center a liquid circulates throughout the entire cord and the ventricles of the brain. The pulsations of the brain pump this fluid which is essential to healthy neural life. Aiding in the circulation is the dura mater, the thick covering of the brain and spinal cord, which attaches to the cranial bones and the spine, all the way down to the sacrum. The spinal cord and brain covering act as an outer tube, aiding pulsation as they stretch and contract with body flexion and extension.

This three-layered brain is also stacked horizontally. The density and compactness of the brain is matched in volume by the surface area of the nerve network. The brain, then, has two poles, cranial and peripheral, connected by a central axis. It is very much like a tree's branch and root systems. In the tree there is nutrient exchange between two different levels of existence, earth and atmosphere. Dark and light communicate, pumping through the trunk the liquids from the tidal pools of the earth and the sun. The brain operates in much the same way.

54 THE THREE NEURAL LAYERS

IMAGE FIFTY-FIVE. The three human brains —the outer cortex, the midbrain with its hollow chambers, and the brain stem and spinal cord with its unifying network of nerves to the arm. Muscle pressure or squeezing or a lack of muscle tone deeply affects the pulsatory quality of the neural organ.

IMAGE FIFTY-SIX. The layers of the brain as human evolution and structured history. The cold-blooded reptilian brain is represented by the geometry of the spinal cord and the bird-serpent shape of the medulla and pons. The middle portion, the thalamic-emotional brain represents the warm-blooded animal-mammal-human. And the cortex represents the human brain, with its transmission of culture, its ability to make symbols and use tools to further human interaction. This image is a modern totem pole, showing our history from creature, to animal, to human.

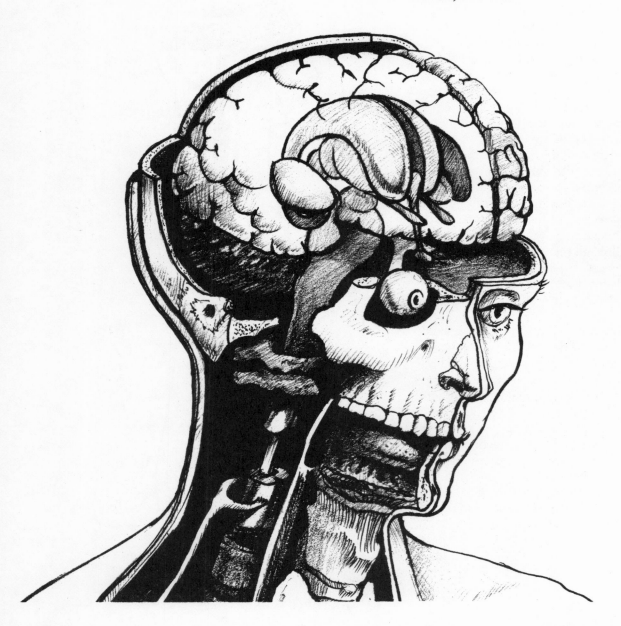

56 **THE TOTEM OF CONSCIOUSNESS**

the invisible layer: liquidity, feeling, hormones, and emotion

water

Water, the basic element of life, is composed of two gases, hydrogen and oxygen. We think of water as a substance but it is more than that, it is a complex arrangement of molecules with a specific growth pattern. A particular regularity, cooling, causes a more dense structure producing ice, a solid. If the molecular structure is heated it opens up and becomes steam. Water is thus capable of being gaseous, liquid, and solid. It is capable of being stored energy, a solid like ice, or potential energy, a gas, or an intermediate form, a liquid. To understand human form, it is essential to understand these properties of water.

The state of liquidity reveals the state of human life. An embryo or an infant is somewhat liquid-like, fragile yet flexible. Growth makes the organism more dense, stringy, solid. Liquidity is bound into flexible packages of hard, impassible, compressed solids that become thicker and calcified in aging and death. Death brings liquification and a gaseous state called decomposition.

Water, a structure of molecular geometry, is capable of electrification. These events generate a current just as the rotational movements of the earth, the processes of heat, or the cold of space generate a current. These forces create various fluids, from bound water to gaseous water, from ice to gas, forming under proper temperatures an electrified fluid that has different properties. Water expands and contracts as it flows. It is able to assume a huge variety of forms. There is excited water, unexcited water, heated water and cold water, still water, and frothy water.

One of the most remarkable liquids is protoplasm, a serum whose dynamics are the basis of organized life. Protoplasm flows, pulses and is capable of reversing its direction of movement. From its own viscosity protoplasm makes membranes and tubes to flow in, and further builds these membranes into cells.

Protoplasm can reverse its direction and become softer or harder. The human body does the same; it becomes muscle bound or flaccid. Fear and anger stiffen the organism, love and caring soften it.

When water becomes electrified, it is capable of behaving differently. It becomes like a battery. Acid water is different from alkaline water. In the evolution of water as life, proteins and steroids were formed. Water became a chemical capable of disolving materials, breaking them down, converting them from one form to another. H_2O became a catalyst, speeding up processes, healing, and synthesizing structure.

Water is a fluid process that transforms itself, making cells with boundaries that evolve further into blood, tissue fluids, lymph, sweat, urine, semen, vaginal fluids, spinal and joint fluids, exhaled water, the digestive juices and hormones. These fluid mixtures are not free-flowing but are stored in cells, pouches, and bladders until expelled by powerful cell and muscle pulsations into tubes or specialized fluids. The pulsations of hormones and enzymes manufacture and help stimulate these specialized fluids.

General pulsation patterns facilitate the specialized work of these fluids such as stimulating growth, producing energy for quick response, and providing oxygenation for growth, stimulating sexual behavior, providing neurological connections. The accordion-like action of the body helps maintain these liquid states. If general pulsation is increased there is a crisis of performance. Overactivity creates exhaustion. If general pulsation is decreased performance is sluggish and depressed. These specialized liquids, then, are responsible for the quality of life. They facilitate biological, emotional, and psychological integration, and produce deep feelings and states of knowledge.

hormones

Hormones are one form of water and are the root of behavior in the animal world. The word hormone means outpouring, having the property to impel or excite. Hormones are excitation in a particularized form, the waters that keep fires burning, the quick fires of epinephrine, the continuing heat of the pituitary, or the continuing transactions of the brain with the neural transmitters.

Hormones are liquid anatomy, the outpourings that convert children into adults. These charged fluids influence growth, making pygmies or giants. The brain is a hormonal gland secreting into the bloodstream magic elixirs. These are the hormones that magnetize the blood, turning boys and girls into men and women, and women into lactating mothers. A sense of growth and warmth comes from the pituitary and thyroid. Feelings of power arise from the adrenal and sexual glands as do the specific urges and responses toward the opposite sex. The deep feelings of the intestines and the heart arise from these hormonal fluids.

Hormones and enzymes give rise to an inner sense of flow and liquidity. The liquid behavior waits to crystalize into muscular behavior. Digestive hormones facilitate intestinal and organ peristalsis. Epinephrine speeds up the heart and calls forth the action of fight or flight, challenge and combat. The gonads and pituitary call out specific sexual motor actions. We creep and crawl with hunger or fear or the excitation to know. We stand, walk, run with the maturation of adrenal excitation, sexual excitation, or the hunger for food.

feelings and emotions

Emotions and feelings follow the rules of water. When we brace ourselves for shock or a blow or when we harden to confine pain, our liquid state is like ice. When we melt with love or dissolve into tears, our feeling state is liquid. Our visceral state gives rise to feelings of hunger, emptiness, yearning, longing, followed by satisfaction and fullness.

Love, caring, attraction, rage, disgust are emotional states that are the subject of our awareness. They are also a readiness for intended action. We emote and are a geyser or a river. We act like a tide or an ice flow. We cascade and stream. We cry and sob, sigh and moan emitting formed fluids. These are the dynamic powers of water finding a way to transform itself into structures and thereby change itself.

Feelings and emotions, hormones, bodies, and consciousness all change form and speak in many tongues. Shapes crystalize and liquify. No one is fixed in concrete; rather some processes are ice or bone-like and others are more fluid.

Liquid life is identified in the language of function, the flow of thought, the tides of feelings, the waves of intuition, the ocean depths of feelings, the waxing and waning of images. Liquids are really a part of the psyche. They are messengers that signal behavior. Their ingredients organize and categorize behavior. Sexual excitation arouses the body and calls out the rituals of courtship.

We are a sea of liquids making a structure and shape, an organismic configuration, a form, a geometry, a pattern of pulsation leading to certain patterns of experienced life, feeling, and thinking both within ourselves and with others.

anatomy as self-identity

To the average layman anatomy is inanimate, it pertains to objects or mechanical events, or is the study of mere matter or corpses. For others the human form is confused with animal forms on either the organ or organismic level. The human heart or brain cannot be compared to that of a rat or a chimpanzee. Human anatomy is a dynamic kinetic and emotional process. Anatomy gives an identity, a specific recognizable shape, and a way of functioning based upon that shape.

The study of the human shape reveals its genetic and emotional history. Shape reflects the nature of individual challenges and how they affect the human organism. Have we stiffened with pride or shrunk with shame? Are we hardened because of deprivation or have we kept safe by collapsing? Does our form indicate a failure to convert feelings into action? Has extended schooling caused overstimulation, a life of sensation, an overactive brain?

The human anatomical form is distinguished by its uprightness and its flexibility. Uprightness is accompanied by an emotional history of parental bondings and separations, closeness and distance, acceptance and rejection. A person may stand with the

compact density that reflects defiance or the sunken chest that expresses shame. Human anatomy is thus more than a biochemical configuration; it is an emotional morphology. Particular anatomical shapes produce a corresponding set of human feelings.

Anatomy is a kinetic morphology, the shapes of human process extended over time. It is a pattern of feeling, a state of tissue. This feeling pattern or tissue state is the feeling of ourselves as individuals capable of expansion and contraction, arousal and satiation. The feeling of ourselves is a by-product of cellular metabolism and tissue tone codified in the brain as the way we function. Thus the shape of the tissue plays a part in determining its own sensations and feelings.

There is a body plan. The various tubes and layers, pouches and diaphragms act together to give a feeling of one's self. Muscle gives rise to sensations of rhythm, containment, holding, releasing, shortening and lengthening. Bone introduces sensations of compression and pulling. The intestines produce sensations of swelling, fullness, and emptying. Empty and dense spaces give rise to other feelings. The uterus, like the heart, is an empty space surrounded by dense, rhythmical tissue. The abdomen is a central cavity containing fluids and organs surrounded by bone and muscle. The lungs and heart are organs which are contained by a rigid wall. Thus hollow, soft, and dense tissue produce different sensations and feelings. There is a dialogue of sensations from hollows to solids, from liquid chambers of the brain to densely packed muscle cells. This overall relationship generates a basic tissue state that forms a continuous pattern of consciousness.

57 THE ARCHITECTURE OF HUMAN EXISTENCE: I

IMAGES FIFTY-SEVEN AND FIFTY-EIGHT. The body plan—human anatomy as a complex layered tube with pouches, sub-pouches, and diaphragms. The layering and tubal concepts are visible: the ectomorphic outer tube of skin and nerves; the mesomorphic middle tube of muscle and bone; the endomorphic inner tube of intestines and lungs. The human organism is tubes within tubes, a triple hourglass image.

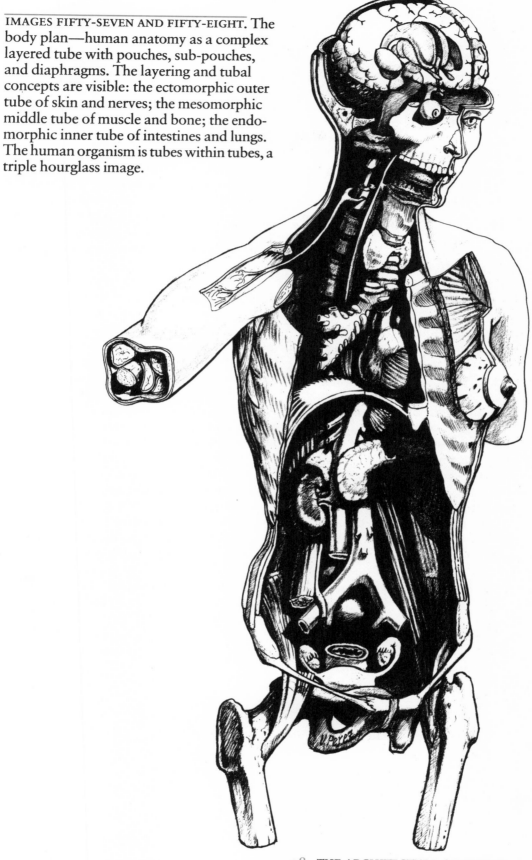

58 THE ARCHITECTURE OF HUMAN EXISTENCE: II

Images 57 and 58 indicate pouches and constrictions. The pouch of the head is open to view. This subdivision at the base of the brain pan contains the foramen magnum, the spinal cord, the ethmoid bone, and the sphenoid bone upon which rests the brain with its fourth ventricle. The second subdivision is the vault that houses the tongue and nasopharynx leading into the trachea. In this upper segment is the constriction called the neck with its air and food passages, the larynx, and the chemoreceptors for the brain's blood supply, the major arteries, the thyroid and subnasale glands. The neck with its brain stem and spinal cord bulge forms a little brain, a powerful accompaniment to the more expanded higher brain. There is the diaphragm of the tongue, foramen magnum, spinal cord, and palate. In the thoracic pouch is the double domed diaphragm with its intersecting vessels—the vagus nerve, esophagus, arteries, veins—and a heart that is quite close to the lungs. You see the upper chest wall layering—internal and external muscles—and how the diaphragm is connected to the chest wall and bounded by the clavicles, sternum, and larynx. Below the thoracic pouch is revealed the abdominal-pelvic vault. The diaphragm attaches to the lower costal margins and is fused with the quadrus and abdominal muscles; the entire organ forms a great sheath. It becomes part of the psoas muscle and external side wall, connects with the illiacus, and thus becomes part of the legs. Observe the pelvic floor with its iliococcygeal and levator ani muscles and the accompanying exits and entrances.

Breathing is an interaction between the pouches and layers. There is a complex pattern of pulsations in each compartment that generates and sustains a force, giving rise to a geometry of sensations and feelings that become tissue consciousness. Each of these segments has a different capacity. The head has a structure for more subtle pulsation, the abdomen for fuller pulsation. The cranial pump is confined to a space that makes for more intense motility while primary respiration in the thoracic cavity has a bellows-like structure.

The body plan, then, consists of layers, tubes, pouches, and diaphragms interacting to produce a pattern of pulsation. The body plan is liquid and emotional motility congealed into shapes for action. When tubes and pouches are rigid, dense, swollen, or collapsed the pulsatory continuum is affected. The relationship between these structures and the accompanying feelings of anguish, fear, anger, defiance, pride, and defeat forms the second half of this book. Yet in Images 57 and 58 the full pulsatory range of elongation, swelling, shortening, and compression is invoked. Here is basic human movement—to extend, to swell, to twist, to shorten, to compress—with accompanying feelings of pride, assertion, holding one's ground, standing upright.

three

insults to form

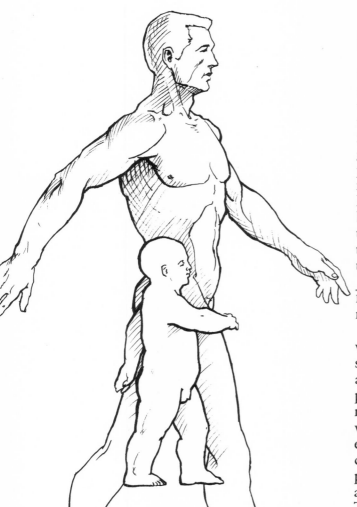

uprightness and insult

FROM A SOMATIC process perspective uprightness is a vertical, pulsatory, emotional wave, capable of extending itself toward the world and contracting itself back. Uprightness is the organization of human experience growing out of the genetic organization of pulsation. Standing erect is often viewed mechanistically. In these interpretations the human stands erect because of good posture, bones resting upon bones, proper gravitational alignment. The role of human interaction and feeling is dismissed in forming an upright self.

IMAGE FIFTY-NINE. Human uprightness: its nature and learning.

Uprightness is based upon the vitality of vertical pulsation, a wave sustained by a support system of tubes, layers, pouches, and diaphragms. In normal functioning the pulsatory wave is capable of a variety of movements, to the world, away from the world. It can speed up and slow down. It enables the organism to give and take, to contain and withhold, to push away and pull toward. These pulsatory movements are the basic organization of our feeling life. They generate excitation, sexual desire, generosity, and love.

Uprightness is a term with a multiplicity of meanings. On one level it is a genetic configuration. On another level it is a bio-chemical environment. It is a mechanical configuration on a third level. At a fourth level it is emotional. It refers to the development from motility to movement and the mastery of the gravitational field. Upright-ness has a symbolic meaning when it refers to the interactions between the child and its parents or society, interactions in which the person inflates or shrinks as a way of dealing with emotional or physical insults.

Uprightness exposes the vulnerability of the human organism. In the animal world, the soft and vulnerable parts of the organism are close to the ground, protected by the hard back and limbs. To show submission in territorial disputes animals turn over to expose their soft front. Instead of meeting the world protected as animals do, humans meet it upright and exposed. This upright stance permanently exposes the soft front to the environment, increasing the surface area of the nervous system and adding to the information provided by the senses of the head—the eyes, ears, nose. With the expo-sure of the soft front more intimate encoun-ters are possible, yet threats and dangers will also be immediately experienced. As the organism defends itself by protecting the softness of its exposed front, uprightness will be affected.

Uprightness, then, is more than standing up. It is an emotional as well as a social event, an internal organization of tubes and layers, pouches and diaphragms in a excita-tory symphony. Human uprightness is a genetic urge, yet, it requires a social and interpersonal network to be realized. Put another way, what nature intended as the development and expression of human form is influenced by personal emotional history.

the startle reflex

The family is a vehicle for completing the development of the human child by provid-ing the care, support, and communication of experience that mitigates the pains and crises of growing to maturity. In addition, the organism is provided with an instinctual reflex to deal with danger and threat. This mechanism, called the startle reflex, is intended for emergencies or short periods of

alarm. We stop, pause, brace, tighten our muscles, hold our breath, investigate and respond by either waiting out the danger or taking action. If the threat is severe or refuses to go away, the startle pattern deepens. We avoid, turn away, prepare to fight or run. If the threat continues further or our previous stances do not reduce the threat, we hide, pull in, yield, or collapse. Ideally, internal or external danger creates a reaction which changes our shape temporarily. When the danger has passed, we return to a state of normal activity. In fact, this is not always what happens. A reaction can persist or increase until it becomes a continuous part of the structure. This continuation of a tem-porary response is called stress.

insults

The development from child to adult involves possible insults from external sources—parents, siblings, peers, or educa-tion. Insults may also arise internally, as when emotional responses overwhelm the organism or excitation is greater than it can handle. From a somatic perspective the term "insults" refers to all the events, internal and external, that invoke the startle reflex. For a newborn baby, loud sounds, bright lights, and unfamiliar events may be insults. To an infant darkness, strange animals, and the temporary absence of a parent might all be insults. Later fights and disagreements with friends and sibling rivalry are potential insults. Insults may arise from our own internal states, feelings of anger, dependency, sexuality, hunger for contact, fears of being left, or imagining a horrible event. Certainly insults may result from family life, how we are treated, the quality of care and affection, the nature of discipline, and the encourage-ment or discouragement of emotional expression. But an insult could also be pro-longed economic hardship in the family, the absence of one of the parents, the effects of war, poverty, divorce, death, or verbal and physical abuse targeted at the child.

Threats, insults, shocks, surprises vary in *timing*—whether they occur early or late in our development; in *number*—whether there are few or many; in *source*—whether they come from outside or are a result of an asymmetrical relationship between internal excitation and individual ability to tolerate it; in *duration*—whether a threat is episodic or continuous; and in *severity*—a threat that is mild, moderate, or intense.

When insults to form occur, excitatory currents are changed and, consequently, so are the shapes we assume. The waves that maintain uprightness are currents of contact, reaching out and coming back. They peak and reverse in a reciprocal relationship. We assert ourselves and retreat, we expand and contract, we swell and diminish. These waves structure us horizontally and vertically as well as circumferentially. Pulsation is a cycle of expansion and contraction, a continuum of compression and release that goes out to the world and returns to the self. Contact and withdrawal have an innate rhythm and an inner necessity to complete their cycle. It is like breathing or the beating heart. Inhalation is followed by exhalation. The heart fills with blood, then expels it throughout the body. Expansion and contraction are the essential pumps of existence. They create the tubal wave of uprightness which gives birth to human feeling.

Insults interrupt the organism. The tubal waves that support uprightness either slow down or speed up in an attempt to maintain a human shape. The startle reflex involves a number of stances which alter the tubal waves of pulsation by freezing them, speeding them up in agitation, or slowing them down in thickening or collapse. We no longer are fully upright and pulsatile. Internal pressure and motility no longer function smoothly. Layers and diaphragms, liquids and tubes are all affected. These interferences may cause feelings of anger, fear, depression, rejection, and rage. If temporary, the pulsatory cycles return to normal. But if insults persist or increase, the structure remains rigid or compact, swollen, or collapsed.

The organism first reacts to insult by becoming more solid. It stiffens itself, organizes more form, becomes rigid then dense. As metabolic processes speed up, organs, the muscle system, and the brain become inflamed. The structure tries to control this increased excitation either by spasticity and bracing or compaction and compression. These conditions are accompanied by feel-

ings of anger, rage, control, defiance, and self-doubt. Solidifying the organism as a way to deal with insults is called overboundedness.

As insults continue and increase, the organism becomes more liquid-like. It loses its shape and becomes swollen or collapsed. The metabolic processes slow down. Excitation either remains at the surface level or dies down to an ember. Organ motility and general excitory peristalsis diminish. There are feelings of inflation, invasiveness, grandiosity, or collapse, despair, helplessness. The structure expands into the world to find a connection to fill it or it collapses inward and shrinks from the world. Becoming more liquid-like in response to insults is called underboundedness.

The startle reaction is a complicated process that begins with simple spontaneous responses to insults or with simple emotional responses to the unknown or to danger. Yet the startle reflex involves a predisposition toward more complex shapes depending upon the timing, the intensity, and the duration of the unknown. With a combination of these conditions the simple reflex becomes a complicated process that permanently affects the individual. Startle, alertness, and the immediate responses of either fight or flight give way to trauma and somatic distress. We remain in an on-going state of preparation for combat, of getting away from what threatens us, or we become weakened or collapsed. We may be in a constant mild brace or a deep spastic rigidity that reflects terror and rage. As these states become permanent, flexibility and responsiveness are lost. This affects all tissues, muscles, organs, and cells as well as thoughts and feelings.

Startle and stress are not the same. Startle is an immediate response whereas stress is the intensification and continuation of responses based on societal and interpersonal interactions. Each person has a unique pattern of insult that could be characterized by the number, the timing and duration, the source, and the severity of the threat posed either physically or emotionally to the organism. It is the number and nature of these factors as well as their interaction that moves an individual from a position of mild startle to one that is more severe. Likewise, it is the unique pattern of insults that an individual receives that turns a temporary startle response into a position of permanent stress. We all meet a number of insults on our way to uprightness, but it is the nature of these assaults as well as our response that is critical in the shaping of form.

The upright organism thus experiences a threat, an insult, an assault. Threats to the person attack the integrity of the support system—how can it maintain uprightness and still deal with what is invasive? This assault is experienced simultaneously on many different levels. On one level, pulsation speeds up or slows down. On another level, there is a continuum of shifts and adjustments to the tender front of the organism. Layers and underlying pouches change. Constrictions that separate the pouches tighten or become looser, creating faster or slower pumping. The balance between tenderness and assertiveness shifts, distorting both. Assertion becomes pride, anger, rage, and terror. Tenderness becomes sadness, grief, helplessness, hopelessness. Uprightness or tubal integrity shifts. First we stiffen or brace to resist invasion, then we densify and compact to protect our internal fire. We then swell our pouches to provide the support the muscles no longer give, and finally, we give in or collapse and retreat to a lower level of functioning. With these shifts feelings change. Distress brings about feelings of fear and anger, dread and anguish, helplessness and loss, despair and depression.

The questions this chapter addresses are: How do emotional insults affect uprightness? How does the startle reflex get invoked? How does the continuation or intensification of an insult invoke a more severe startle position? How does the startle reflex get perpetuated as a pattern of stress? How do startle or stress patterns influence tubes, layers, pouches, diaphragms and pulsation? How does a permanent change in shape come about? How does a change in shape become a change in feeling?

insults, alarm, and stress

As we face the world we are upright. The soft front of the body is exposed. We are prepared to move out of ourselves into the world or from the world into ourselves. Insults temporarily invoke the startle reflex; it may be perpetuated as stress. Uprightness and our move toward the world is interrupted. We attempt to preserve our humanity by defending ourselves.

We are programmed with the startle reflex, a series of alarm responses lying along a continuum. The startle reflex begins with an investigative response, followed by assertion, then an annoyance reaction, then anger or avoidance, and, finally, submission and collapse. If the first response alleviates the insult, the event that interrupts us, the organism returns to homeostasis. If not, the first response can invoke the second, the second lead to the third, and so on. In cases of severe threat, the early stages of startle are by-passed and we jump immediately to a more extreme response. Yet the continuum of startle responses does not necessarily occur in an invariable order; neither are the steps sequential. One or several steps could be by-passed.

IMAGE SIXTY. Four of the startle responses, viewed in a clockwise sequence. These four startle responses show variations depending upon the nature of the event, temporary or continuous, mild or severe. The center position represents normal activity before insult occurs. When initially surprised the response is to investigate, challenge, straighten up, become more erect. The 12 o'clock position shows this uprightness as a readiness for action. In the 3 o'clock position the response is to rigidify, brace, hyper-extend, pull back. This stance reflects fear, anger, attack. The response at the 9 o'clock position is to flex forward, close up, pull in. This stance is self-protective. At the 6 o'clock position the response is collapse, falling inward. This stance is to become invisible or unconscious.

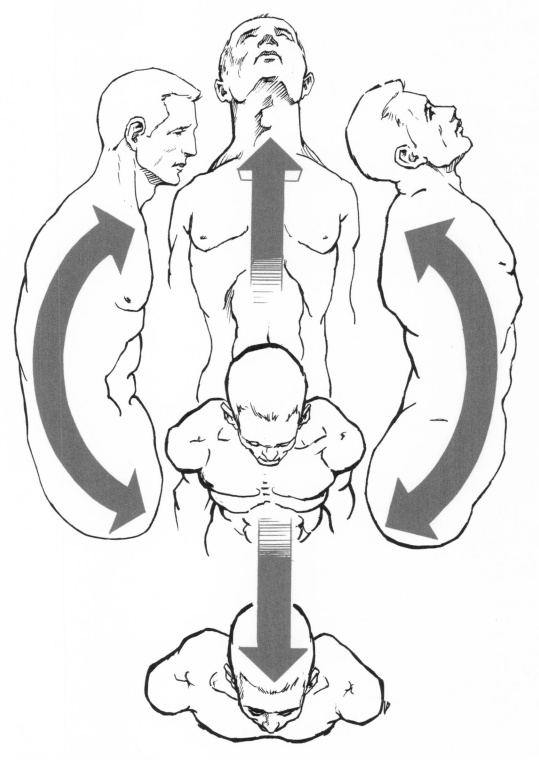

60 FOUR STARTLE RESPONSES

The startle response is an organismic response to deal with emergency situations. It is meant to be used temporarily; when the danger passes the organism returns to normal. However, this same response can become a habitual state, so that its organization remains as we move from event to event. It does not get disorganized but remains as a continuous somatic pattern. Many people are always in a state of moderate brace against a danger that they can't fully articulate. The word "stress" is used to describe this ongoing state, whereas "startle" or "alarm" refers to the temporary state. The images used throughout this chapter refer to dynamics which are organismically similar in both the startle and stress situations.

The startle reflex is the fundamental response to any stimuli that are unknown, whether the stimuli be painful or pleasurable. It commits our attention to the new stimuli by pulling us from present activity. This reflex both de-focuses and refocuses attention instantaneously and thereby protects the organism by telling it what is there, either inside or outside.

The startle response begins in the upper half of the body. In the first stage of startle, rigidity, the spine straightens out, perhaps even arches. All the spinal extensor muscles contract. This is paradoxical because the reaction to fear is flexion, folding the body inward to protect the internal organs. Flexion involves the strong muscles of the back. But in the first startle response flexion doesn't occur, extension does. This isolates the stimulus and focuses on it. To focus the upper body must grab, hold, brace. So the beginning of the startle reaction can be characterized as a state of "hold it!" Everything stops. Everything is in a state of alertness. The first steps involve stiffening the spine, descent of the diaphragm, opening the airways, and grabbing the lungs.

In the continuum of responses from mild caution to severe shock or terror, the degree of rigidity increases until it anesthetizes the organism. In an extreme state of shock there is total immobility of the muscles, spinal cord, and the lungs, a defocusing of the eyes, and a partial congealing of the fluids and the arterial blood supply. This occurs in animals when they are attacked by their enemies.

In the beginning stages of startle all the teleceptors—the eyes, ears, nose—are highly alert. Where is the danger, what is it, does it trigger associations? A newborn child is without associations so it immediately cries for help. In the last and most extreme state, shock, the small muscles and smooth muscles of the organism lock. Anesthetization occurs. This state can be preceded by fainting, falling, or collapsing. Blood pressure drops, the organism completely withdraws from its surfaces into its depths and retreats to the deepest recesses of life. Extreme shock and loss of blood pressure can sometimes result in death. So rigidity and shock are the extremes; one is mild, the other is severe. And there are many positions in between.

The startle reflex is based upon the ability of the organism to halt pulsation, create segmentation, and recruit more and more layers of itself to its response. The startle reflex involves:

a) a change in the musculature and posture,
b) a change in the diaphragm's shape,
c) a thickening or thinning of the body wall,
d) an increase in the separations between the pouches,
e) a change in the body's relationship to the earth's gravitational line,
f) an alteration of feelings, emotions, and thinking.

IMAGE SIXTY-ONE. Investigation, caution —the beginning of the startle reflex. Inhibition ends present activity and alerts and braces us to investigate, to be in our senses, to search, to discover what is there. Insults increase alertness, organizing attention and readiness for action. There is mild adrenalization. This state is not necessarily negative. Actors, speakers, athletes, and students utilize this basic pattern. This state is considered desirable in competition and performance. It appears to be more than our ordinary state, causing alertness with its accompanying arousal, yet without the fear of combat. To be alert yet non-combative is rare because arousal mobilizes the fight-flight muscles. Tubes become attentive and stiff and lift up slightly from the pelvis. There is increased excitatory activity, and an increase in muscle tone. Pouches expand and organ motility increases. The abdominal-pelvic pouch compresses slightly while the thoracic and cranial pouches puff up. Peristalsis thus increases. Skeletal muscle pulls us upward in order to make us alert. The mouth closes, the nostrils flare, the eyes open, the head is stilled, the hands are ready to open, the arms flex, while the chest is raised by the intercostals, the diaphragm descends, and the legs stiffen slightly. In short, the outer wall compresses but the cavities remain undisturbed. There is arousal in the brain; attention is free flowing. This is a territorial stance of protecting one's ground.

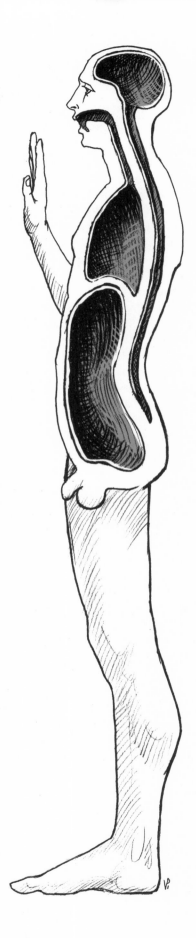

IMAGE SIXTY-TWO. Bracing, Dislike, Pride. Distress begins here. The abdominal pouch compresses while the upper pouch expands. The diaphragm descends. Tubes brace. The chest raises, inspires; the intestines tighten; senses focus on the object; the structure braces even more. Excitation intensifies and organ pulsation increases. The organism pulls out of the pelvis and off of the ground. The statement of this stance is "keep your distance or I will attack." The "stay there" position is seen in the extended palm, the danger position is evidenced by the closed fist, and the bluff position is seen in the body making itself bigger. The muscles of the abdominal-pelvic cavity increase their pressure, squeezing force into the chest and head. Pulsations compartmentalize, increase and deepen in the chest, decrease in the intestines. The arms, legs, feet, and muscles contract, ready to push, hit, dig in, freeze, become still, or hold tight. This is the stance of dislike, of making boundaries.

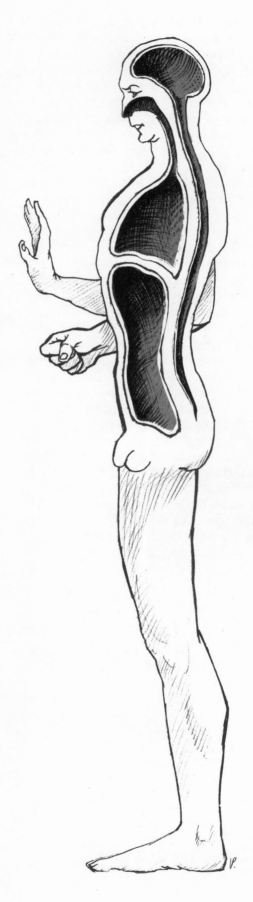

62 BRACING, DISLIKE, PRIDE

IMAGE SIXTY-THREE. Rigidity, aversion, fear. Up to this point the startle/stress response has involved facing forward, confronting what is; it is oriented toward the world. The organism has been expansive, alert, elongated, attentive. Here the aversion pattern begins in a readiness to turn away from an attack response. The organism is in conflict, unsure whether it is facing forward, turning, or folding into a ball. This results from compression in the abdominal wall and the viscera, a shift toward the head which is now deeply suffused with blood, and the innate tendency to fold up in defense. The program to grab with the mouth and hands also lifts the body off the ground. The cavities of the head and chest greatly expand. Motility increases in the head and thorax. The abdominal organs are pressurized with decreased motility and blood flow. The pelvis and feet pull up severely. Excitation speeds up. Tubes contract and congeal on their way to becoming solid. The message is "you go or I will go." We lose control of our surround, of affecting the other. We are trapped and cannot get out. We stay in the situation but begin to dissociate. This is the beginning of disorganization.

IMAGE SIXTY-FOUR. Bracing and spasticity. Here compression, spasticity, and solidity begin. The organism cannot move, cannot do anything, freezes up, caught in upward extension. It says, "I won't be a threat, I won't move, I won't give up or lose my ground." Helplessness arises. The head cavity narrows, the chest locks in inspiration, the intestines become spastic and immobile as the organism totally pulls out of the pelvis and off of the ground. The diaphragm locks in expiration while the chest locks in inspiration. Excitation diminishes. The cranial cavity and spinal cord tube constrict. Cranial pulsation becomes limited as the head severely pulls back and the throat and nasal tubes constrict. The hands freeze in the gesture of submission. They lock or brace without any action—a signal of no contact. Rather than arousal there is suspended animation. This is the beginning of increased fragmentation with panic and crying responses.

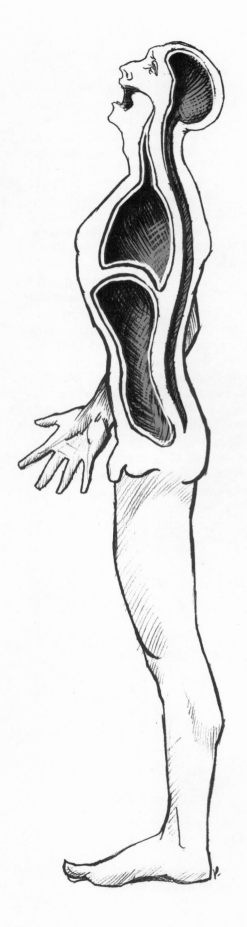

64 BRACING, SPASTICITY

IMAGE SIXTY-FIVE. Withdrawal, submission. Disorganization, descent, and defeat begin. The organism is fatigued, unable to fight. It retreats from the independent warrior stance to the abdominal and visceral pouches. These pouches expand while pulsation in the chest and head becomes sluggish. Chest pressure deflates. The diaphragm begins to descend, the chest collapses. Tubes become weak and sag. The pouches lose their vitality, become irregular, lacking support. The upper cavities of the cranium, chest, esophagus drag downward with the collapse of the anterior abdominal wall. The abdominal wall stretches due to weakness. Excitation is depressed. We no longer have hope or expect help, support, encouragement, or contact. We sink into a state of submission. The statements are "I give in, I submit, I shrink."

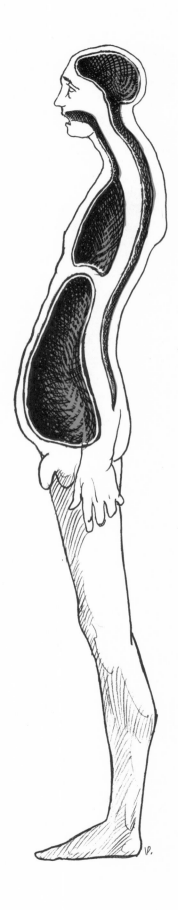

IMAGE SIXTY-SIX. Collapse, defeat, resignation. The abdominal and cranial organs become flaccid while the oral and digestive tube become spastic. The abdominal-pelvic pouch collapses or bulges out. The diaphragm flattens in the position of expiration, yet, paradoxically, the chest is deflated. Because of fatigue there is little or no excitation; rather there is apathy, resignation, a lack of confidence. Respiration occurs through belly breathing because the upper chest no longer moves easily. The protrusion of the intestines signifies poor pulsation and peristalsis. The buckling of the legs furthers the tendency to collapse. The head, spine, esophagus, and tongue pull down with the prolapse of the abdominal organs which swell to provide support. We give up trying and feel despair, apathy, defeat, terror, and hopelessness. The emotional statement is "I cave in, resign myself, cease to exist."

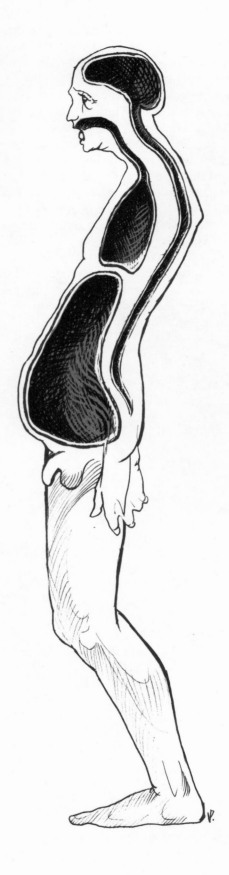

66 COLLAPSE, DEFEAT, RESIGNATION

IMAGE SIXTY-SEVEN. Frozen terror, extreme startle. This response is not part of the continuum but an instantaneous result in cases of extreme shock. It is the Morro reflex. In this stance, seen occasionally in children, there is instant shrinking and fragmentation, a splitting as if the organism were flying apart. All the cavities—head, chest, mouth, abdomen—instantly narrow. Motility is at a minimum. Activity freezes. The limbs become spastic. The breathing is held in the expiratory position. Withdrawal takes place by a retreat into coma.

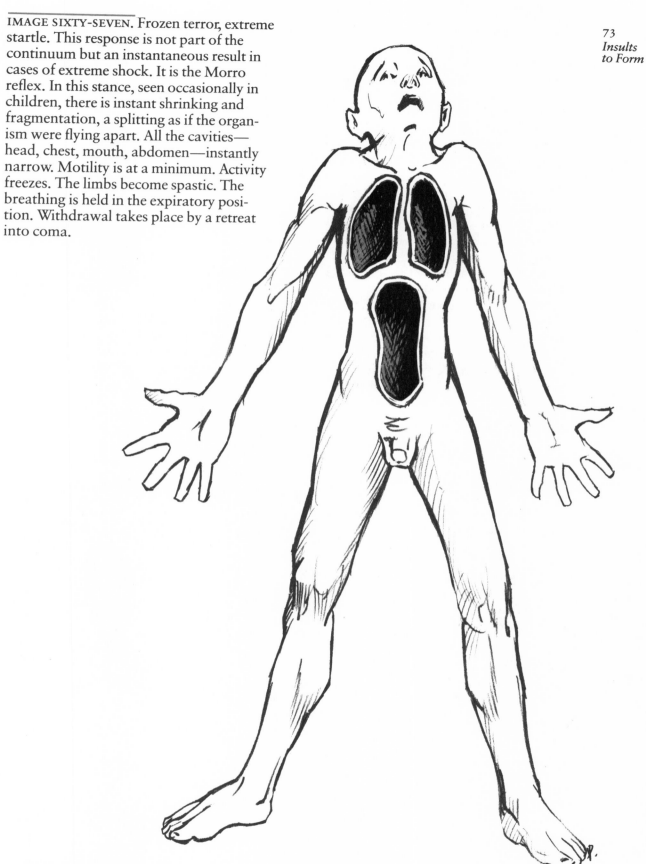

67 FROZEN TERROR, EXTREME STARTLE

IMAGE SIXTY-EIGHT. The startle reflex continuum. This image shows the startle/stress responses as a continuum in which segments progressively stiffen and pouches compress. Holding in the deep layers of the striated muscles is replaced by contraction of the smooth muscles of the intestines, and finally a deep holding of the neural tube resulting in anesthesia and unconsciousness. The startle/stress continuum reveals that the organism first pulls itself upward, separates its upper half from its lower half, pulls itself out of the abdominal-pelvic world into the chest, diaphragm, throat, and brain. This separation later causes real segmentation—splitting the organism into the upper and lower halves. This occurs in response to either an external or an internal fear. Segmentation also happens when rotation or turning away occurs. The organism turns away from itself or others, but if it can't do this the body goes in two directions—it stays put yet goes away. It is

torn. Muscles go in opposite directions. Or it becomes so compressed that living space diminishes, the ability to fill up and swell is gone. The organism ends up one dimensional. Yet the deep urge to elongate remains, so, again, we are at war between full uprightness and collapse.

The startle responses are usually progressive. As an insult either fails to go away or gets stronger, we move along the continuum. Yet, if the insult is overwhelming in the beginning, we may jump along the continuum from investigation to depression or shock. The startle reflex is not mechanistic but complicated and individualized.

Startle or stress responses may also be in conflict. At one level the organism wishes to sag, but at another, it stiffens or braces because collapse itself is an insult. We may be angry at an insult, yet our level of anger may itself be a further assault, so we withdraw and collapse. The startle reflex is not

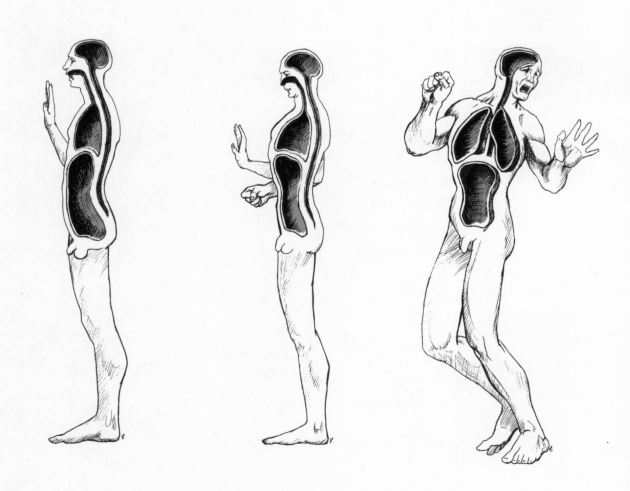

simple; it is possible to have two patterns going on at the same time.

Image 68 reflects two phenomena—the startle reflex patterns and the stress patterns. The former are temporary and utilized for emergencies. The latter are the continuation, intensification, and solidification of startle positions into stress tissue states. The startle/stress continuum visually indicates that two processes are at work—expansion, lengthening, going outward, and contraction, compression, going inward. The first half of the startle positions—Images 61, 62, 63—involve getting bigger; this lengthening can become fixed and unyielding—a stress position. The second half of the startle positions—Images 64, 65, 66—focus on getting smaller; this shortening can become fixed or inevitable—other stress positions.

These somatic patterns are processes of deep self-perception—a way of feeling and knowing the world. They are more than mechanical. They are a form of intelligence, a continuum of self-regulation. These patterns are layered and tubal phenomena that affect the entire organism. They are intrinsic and invoke muscular states from the tip of the head to the toes. Muscles and organs are not just contracted, they are organized into a configuration. These organizations become the way we recognize the world as well as ourselves, and in turn, they become the way the world recognizes us. To understand an individual, then, requires the ability to ascertain what startle or stress configuration may be dominant and what other complex ones may be present, how they affect the person somatically and emotionally, and what they give rise to in terms of self-visions, self-perceptions and self-images.

68   THE CONTINUUM OF STARTLE AND STRESS: FROM ASSERTION TO DEFEAT

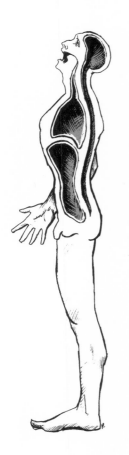
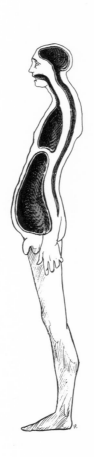
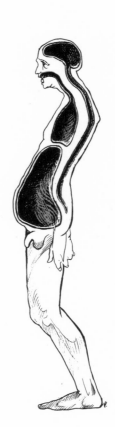

overbound and underbound: the embodying of the stress experience

The organism deals with continuing and accumulative insults in one of two ways. It either resists or gives in. Resistance requires the organism to stand against the attack, to ward it off. Giving in requires the organism to yield, accept the insult and retreat to a lower level of functioning. In resisting the organism becomes more solid; it stiffens or braces. In creating more form, structure, boundaries and solidity the organism becomes over-bound. In giving in the organism softens, yields, becomes more liquid-like. In creating less form, structure, boundaries and a more liquid-like state the organism becomes underbound.

Motility and pulsation are intimately related to the state of tubes, layers, pouches and diaphragms. When these have good tone, that is, uninterrupted motility, it is reflected in physical and emotional vitality. Startle and stress reflexes inhibit motility and pulsation. They create a conflict between the urge to continue the pulsatory pattern and the need to slow it down or speed it up. In order for pulsation to slow down or speed up, the expansive-contractive cycle in tubes, layers, and pouches must be altered.

Pulsation is a continuum of expansion and contraction. Tubes, layers, pouches, and diaphragms set the limit for expansion and contraction. They have a normal range and an emergency range they draw upon temporarily. For example, the heart speeds up when we engage in physical exercise; when we cease exercise the heart returns to normal. Stress responses fixate the organism somewhere along a range of emergency responses—inflamed or inhibited. Since pulsation involves an interaction of the tubes, layers, pouches, and diaphragms, as pulsation speeds up or slows down, the entire organism is affected. Continued long enough, the result is a permanent change in organ and layer shape and functioning.

The startle-stress responses exaggerate the nature of expansion and contraction. The first three startle-stress positions intensify normal expansion, the movement of the self outward and toward the world. The latter three positions distort normal contraction, the movement of the self inward and away from the world. When the expansion-contraction cycle remains fixed or static, somatic shape becomes overbound or underbound.

Overbound refers to the first half of the stress continuum, structures which first brace and stiffen and then compress and compact as a defense against continual insults. Becoming more solid is the first line of defense against stress. To increase form is to become overbound. The result is decreased motility and permeability as well as decreased vulnerability. Excitation becomes depressed, pulsations and peristalsis hibernate.

Underbound refers to the latter half of the stress continuum, structures which first swell into the environment and then collapse inward as a defense against continual insult. Underbound structures become more liquid-like. They create less form as a way to deal with stress. Motility and permeability increase but lack intensity. Excitation leaks out. Pulsation becomes arhythmic and meandering. There is a lack of focus and containment.

IMAGE SIXTY-NINE. The belts: controls for pulsation. Just as pipes have valves to prevent backflow and move things along, so the organism has parts which narrow to move things faster, or widen to slow things down. By increasing or decreasing the valve function, the organism speeds up or slows down.

In response to stress the organism increases or decreases pressure. Pressure changes involve two events occurring simultaneously. First, the layers become more solid or more liquid-like. Second, the pouches move closer together or farther apart. These changes to the layers and pouches change the functioning of the diaphragms and thus, pulsation. The diaphragms are the major exists, entrances, and transition points. These are the places of taking in, letting out, letting something go through, letting something go down, letting something come up, letting something out. The belts illustrate circumferential conflict and how inner spaces are distorted. They show places where holding or compression occurs or where it doesn't, where regulation of pressure and segment specialization occurs. For example, some people pull in their neck until the differentiation between head and thorax is lost. Others constrict their waists to separate abdomen from pelvis. Swelling is an alternate defense. With no minimal constriction, pouches fuse. Image 69 suggests, therefore, that tightening belts increases pulsation, loosening belts decreases pulsation. Tightening some belts, while loosening others, creates erratic pulsation.

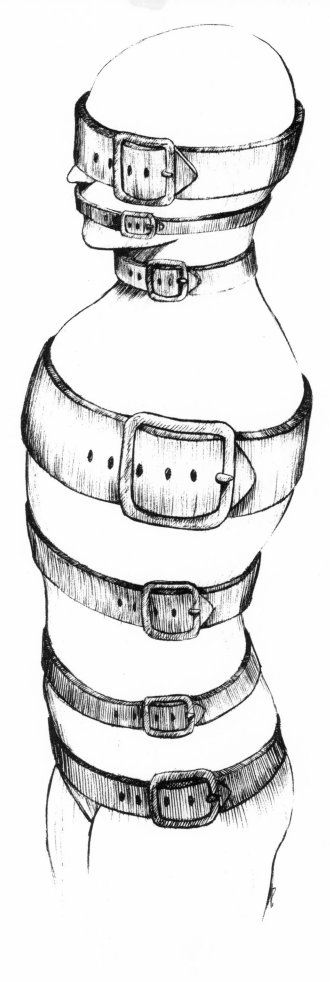

IMAGE SEVENTY. Over and under arousal. When the responses to stress become fixated, organ shapes and motility become distorted. Movement and emotional patterns are affected. Pressure is regulated by the skeletal muscle wall layers which act as a huge diaphagm around a series of pouches. Each pouch has a body wall, a roof, a floor—all acting in concert as a pumping diaphragm. All of the pouches pulsate in a concert of expansion and contraction providing the basic motility that is our self-reference. this pulsatory tide moves back and forth between arousal and containment, expansion and contraction, swelling and shrinking—an accordion-like function. When stress patterns become permanent the pulsatory accordion fails to complete its cycle and becomes locked in inflamed or inhibited arousal. Image 70 depicts the two distortions of normal pulsation: the overbound on the left and the underbound on the right. The overbound speed up pulsation, the underbound slow it down. Pulsation changes when the organism over-expands or over-contracts. In the overbound states stiffening is over-expansion, bracing is over-contraction. In the underbound states swelling is over-expansion, collapse is over-contraction. Image 70 further shows that these patterns are layered; both the muscular tube and the visceral tube are involved. A pattern may exist at both layers. For example, one layer of rigidity covers another rigid layer or collapse exists on top of collapse. Yet alternate stress patterns could be found on top of one another. There might be a rigid middle with a collapsed inner layer or the opposite, a collapsed middle with a rigid interior.

Layers and pouches are involved in how pulsation changes. To speed up pulsation, layers become more solid and pouches come closer together. As the organism fixates in this stance pulsation speeds up more, thus layers must become more solid. The pattern intensifies further. This is equally true in slowed down pulsation, where the layers become less solid and the pouches separate. The remainder of this chapter displays the effects on the pouches, muscles, and tubes of speeded up or slowed down arousal.

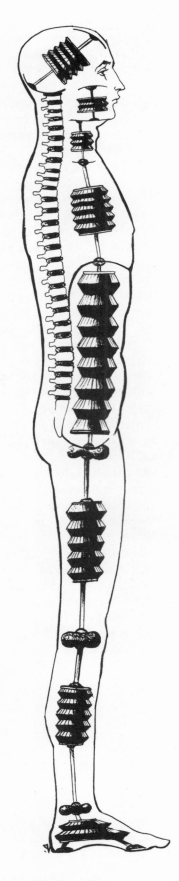

70 PULSATORY DYSFUNCTIONS: GENERALIZED OR LOCALIZED

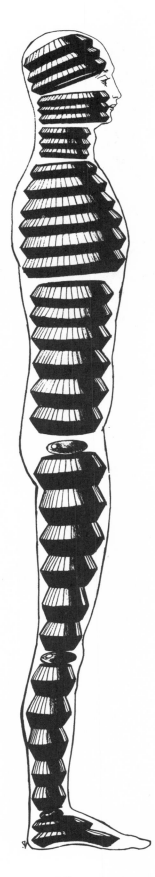

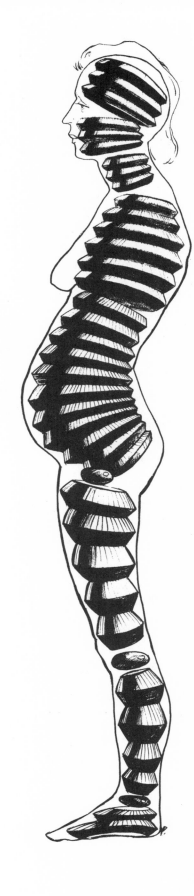

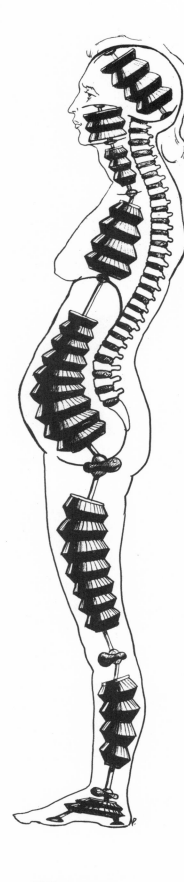

OVERBOUND   UNDERBOUND

IMAGE SEVENTY-ONE. Contained, overbound and underbound pouches. A side view of the major pouches—the head, chest, and pelvis—and the relationships of the three tubes—the skin or outer tube, the middle supportive structure of muscle, and the internal tube or deep organ layer. This image shows the effect of overboundedness and underboundedness on internal organs and tubes.

Distorted relationships occur in the outer wall as well as in the internal organs and the pouches. In overbound structures, rigid and dense people, the cranial vault fills up. The outer walls thicken and encroach inward. The hollows of the inner tube narrow, as do the exits and entrances of the esophagus, aorta, heart, and anus-urethra. Internal pressure builds up. This creates feelings of being trapped or stuffed. The flexibility of the outer wall diminishes. Excitation is depressed, pulsation is stunted, peristalsis intensifies but flattens. All three layers are involved in this complex process. It is also possible, however, for only one layer, outer or inner, to become overbound.

The underbound form, swollen or collapsed structures, develops a thinning of the outer wall. Without muscular resistance, the internal tubes and spaces cannot sustain themselves and begin to either spread outward or collapse inward. Sphincter tone is lost. There is swollenness or prolapse. The heart and lungs expand with fluid. This expansion is noticeable in all the entrances and exits, layers and pouches. As resistance is lost, peristalsis is affected —excitation leaks or meanders without direction or focus. Since the organism is layered, it is equally possible to have swelling on the muscular layer with spasticity as an internal compensation.

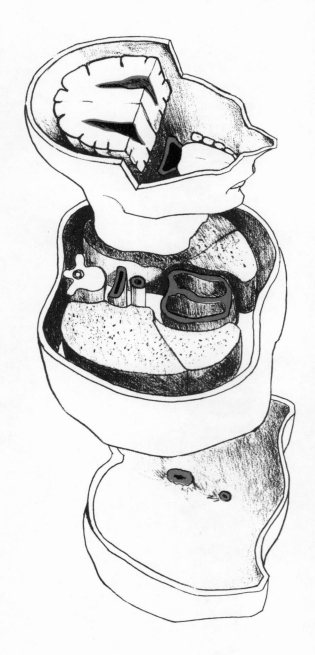

CONTAINED

71 CONTAINED, OVERBOUND, UNDERBOUND POUCHES: A COMPARISON

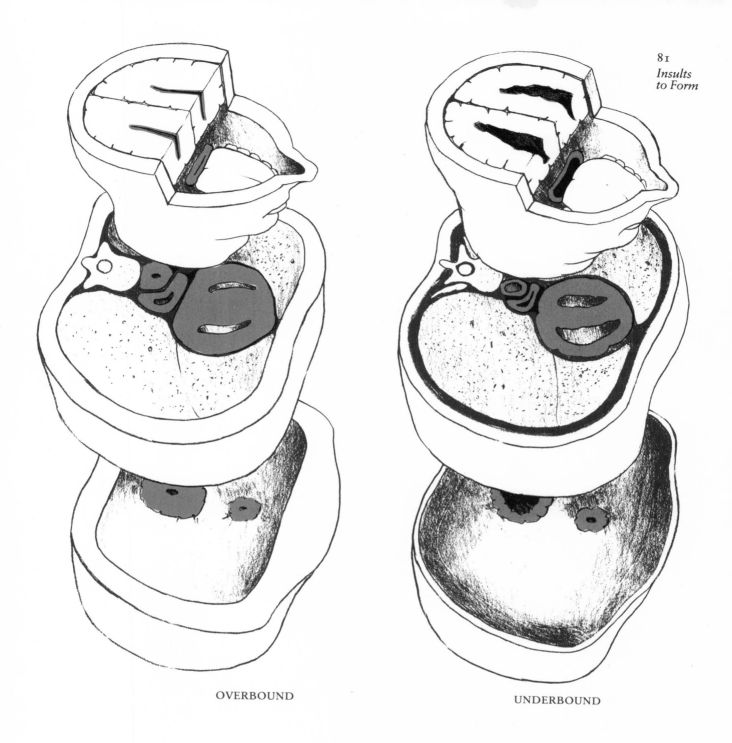

OVERBOUND   UNDERBOUND

IMAGE SEVENTY-TWO. Muscle tone—normal, overbound, underbound. A major function of muscle is to create the tonus which maintains internal boundaries or containers. Normal, or contained muscle, is elastic, capable of full expansion and contraction. The muscle feels firm, smooth, with flexibility and resilience.

Overbound muscle has too much resistance. It is too solid. Rigid muscle is shortened, spastic, narrowed, tight, stringy, knotted. As the muscles over-expand, normal contraction is disrupted. The muscles rigidify like a taut steel cable. Density, the other form of overboundedness, involves muscles that thicken and compact. They become incapable of further compression, like the hemp rope used by ships. This distorts normal expansion. Both these states reflect hypertrophy, over-use, a chronic condition.

Underbound muscle creates too little resistance. As this boundary function weakens, contents swell or leak out. Swollen muscles are water-logged. They appear bloated as if they were filled with liquid, fat, air. There is pressure internally but, as the muscles lack tone, pressure meets little resistance. This distorts normal contraction. Weak or collapsed muscle empties of fluids; it dries out and becomes narrow, spongy, small, tough. It lacks substance and feels as if it has crumbled. There is weakness and atrophy. Both normal expansion and contraction are affected. Both these states reflect hypotrophy and hypoplasia, incomplete tissue development or the loss of function.

Each of these states in its own way disrupts the pumping action of muscle. Rigid muscles have difficulty contracting, dense muscles in expanding. The organism ends up inflexible. Swollen or collapsed unbound muscles can't provide the boundaries that help generate pressure or contain it. The organism leaks out or collapses.

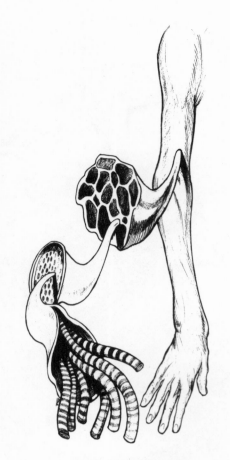

COLLAPSED

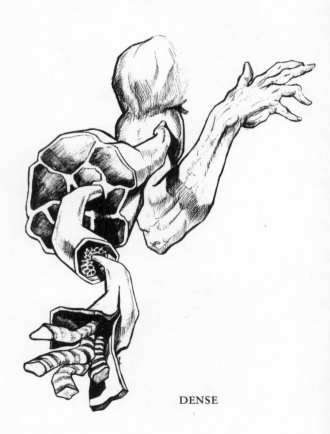

DENSE

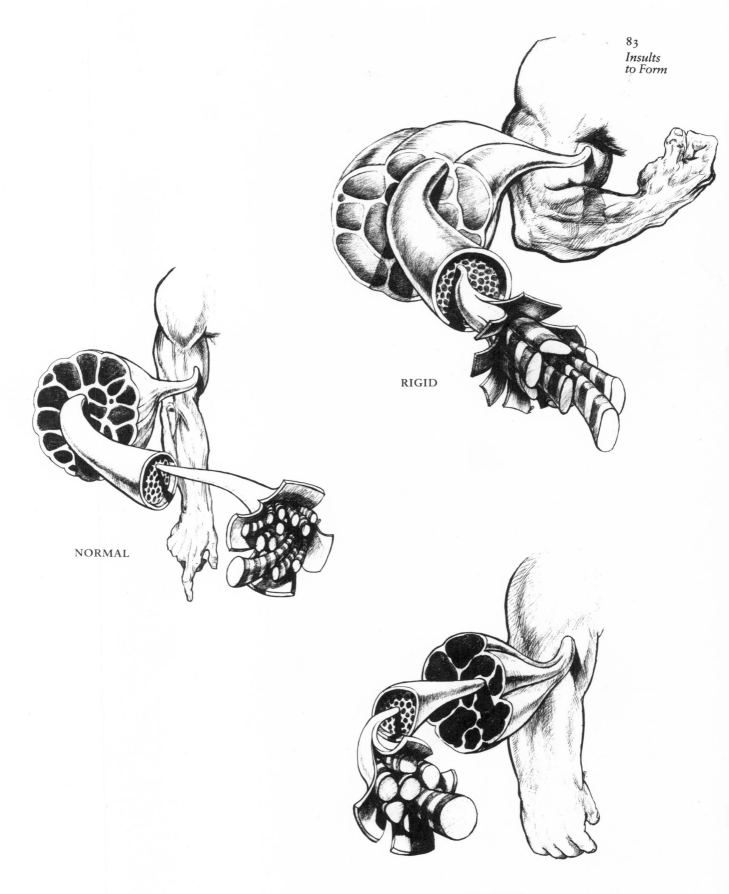

RIGID

NORMAL

SWOLLEN

IMAGE SEVENTY-THREE. Tubes—overbound or underbound. The organism is a series of interconnected tubes—a nutritive tube, surrounded by a muscular tube, encased in a neural tube. A continual pattern of stress distorting any one tube has repercussions on all the other tubes. A rigid muscle tube narrows, becomes angular, tight, stringy, elongated. The tube wall stiffens. There is little recoil or flexibility. The dense tube compacts. The internal hollow is, thus, obliterated inward by an implosion of the tissue. This compacting occurs in both the vertical and outer posterior dimensions. The tube wall thickens; it has poor recoil, little flexibility. An example would be a muscle so imploded that it compresses the blood vessels. The swollen tube expands outward from the inside. The walls of the tube are too flexible; they are thin and weak and yield without any recoil. Without a container the internal contents swell into the surround. The collapsed tube is a weakened structure. The hollow sinks inward since there is no support from the middle tube. All of the tubes are weak and unable to support uprightness. Flexibility and recoil are minimal.

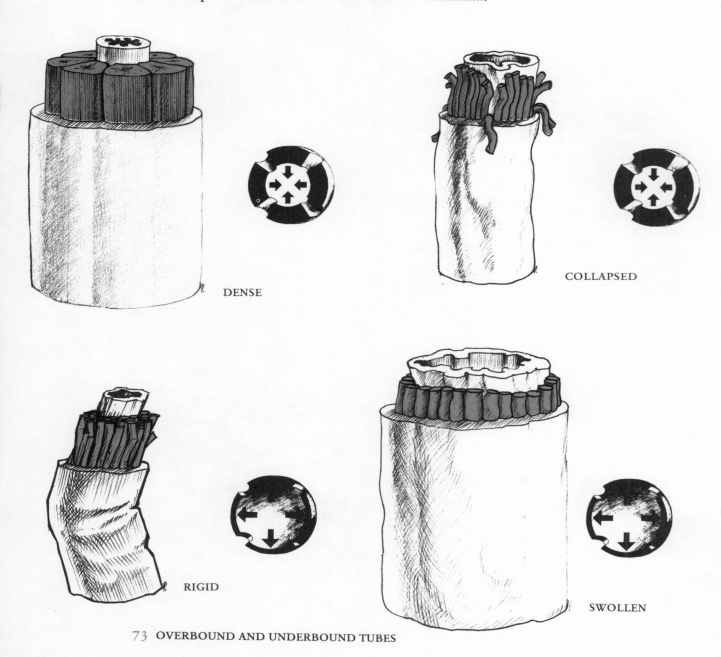

DENSE

COLLAPSED

RIGID

SWOLLEN

73 OVERBOUND AND UNDERBOUND TUBES

IMAGE SEVENTY-FOUR. The interior tubes of cardiac and smooth muscle. Tubes influence one another. A distortion in one tube will have an impact on the adjoining tube. For example, if the muscles and bone tube can't support the organism, the smooth muscle tube might pressurize to provide a support function. The internal tubes and organs are affected by overbound and underbound muscle states. Inside of cardiac and smooth muscle tubes are holes, channels or lumina through which food, air, and blood pass. The esophagus, intestines, bronchial passage, aorta, and vagus nerve are examples of tubes whose internal contents may be influenced by changes in the muscle wall. With rigidity, these holes narrow in spasm. In dense structures a thickened body wall squeezes the holes inward, narrowing them. In swollen structures the muscle tube cannot create resistance. The internal tube inflates and expands. The lumina inside the various tubes lose shape and differentiation. In collapse or atrophy the body wall implodes, crumbles, loses form. Tubes lose some of their shape and form. The lumina are no longer able to remain completely open; they also lose shape and fold inward. Thus interior tubes and the passage of their contents are affected by the increasing or decreasing pressure of the external tubes.

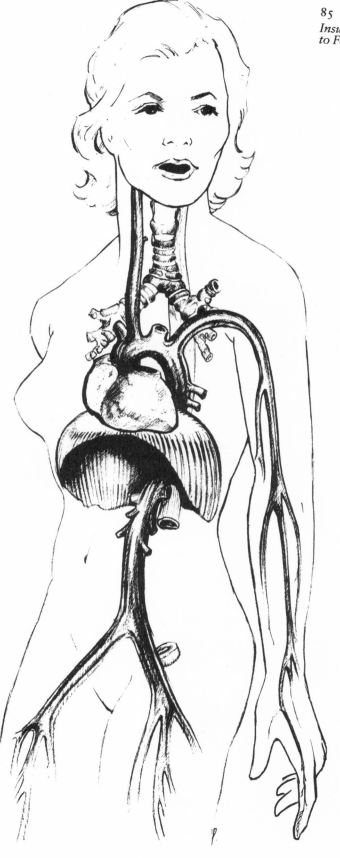

75 THE ROLE OF THE BRAIN: A DIALOGUE
OF TISSUE CONSCIOUSNESS

IMAGE SEVENTY-FIVE. The role of the brain:
a three-level dialogue in the organization of
pulsation. The brain localizes and categor-
izes cellular experience into a general pattern of tissue consciousness. When the pulsation pattern changes, both feeling and cellular shape are altered, as are conscious and
unconscious images and states. In the architecture of the brain there are various parts
which carry on a dialogue to regulate pulsation. The brain stem—the cold-blooded
reptilian brain—regulates primary reflex
actions. It includes primary emotions—fear,
attack, anger. In the midbrain the warm-
blooded, mammalian feelings are laid down
along with the history of caring and contact.
In the outer layer, the cortex, the information and symbol-making functions occur.
Here societal images and emotional messages form a language to regulate the mid-
brain function.

To record tissue consciousness and emotional experiences the three levels of the
brain engage in a dialogue. Startle patterns
start as reflex action, raw patterns of sensation, as the organism becomes alert and stiffens. The mid-brain adds to the dialogue by
invoking past emotional learnings which add
to the survival oriented fight-flight patterns.
Finally, the cortex engages in the conversa-
tion with its input concerning societal and
emotional responses.

Tube layers are represented in the brain as
experience and action possibilities. Startle
and stress, like pleasure and tenderness, are
recorded in the shape of the tubes and
pouches and their cellular state. Image 75
shows how stress and distress experiences
are recorded, how emotion and logic are
formed as responses to hurt, and how these
become a way of thinking and feeling which
lessens pain and encourages survival.

IMAGE SEVENTY-SIX. Mixed types. The previous overbound and underbound examples
represent classic or pure types. Some individuals fall easily into these categories;
others are mixed types. A mixed type is a
structure that is both overbound and underbound. This is the result of two different
stress patterns occurring at different times in
the organism's development. Mixed types
could be found in different pouches or at
different layers. A structure could be weak
in the lower half because it lacked security
when young, but its upper half could be
powerful. A collapsed chest might be offset
by a rigid, dense lower body. A swollen upper
half could be matched with a stubborn, passive, unresponsive lower body. There could
be deep spasticity in the outer layers yet
weakness or swollenness in the inner layers.
On the surface a structure may be defiant
and unyielding, yet on a deeper level it lacks
support and fears collapse.

The first mixed type is contained or normal in the head, rigid in the chest, and swollen in the abdomen. In the second example,
a rigid head is matched with a swollen chest
and a contained abdomen. The final example
is a swollen head matched with a contained
chest and a rigid abdomen.

When one segment is constricted and
another swollen there is mixed sensation
and feeling. Feeling can be trapped, frozen,
dead in one pouch, while it is diffuse, empty,
weak in another. The inside structure could
be anesthetized, rigid, fearing loss of control
while the outside has a full range of expansion and contraction. In mixed types all layers are affected by the swelling or constriction of the various pouches.

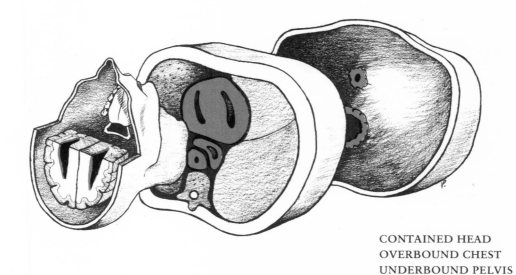

CONTAINED HEAD
OVERBOUND CHEST
UNDERBOUND PELVIS

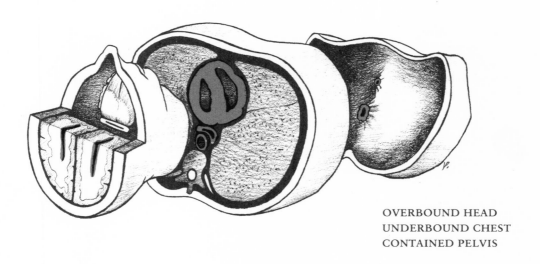

OVERBOUND HEAD
UNDERBOUND CHEST
CONTAINED PELVIS

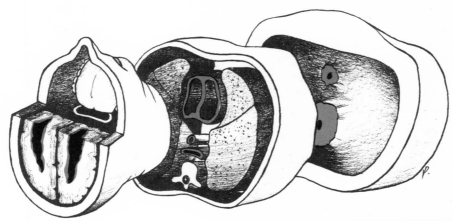

UNDERBOUND HEAD
CONTAINED CHEST
OVERBOUND PELVIS

76 MIXED TYPES: CONTAINED,
OVERBOUND, UNDERBOUND

IMAGE SEVENTY-SEVEN. The layering of the organism. Various layers of the body may simultaneously be in opposite holding patterns. Any tube can be overbound or underbound. The digestive system, muscles, and brain may be agitated while the outer skeletal muscles are inhibited or inactive. One tube is excited, the other subdued, maybe even apathetic. There could be rigidity in the skin or nervous system layer. The digestive tube could be swollen while the muscular layer is collapsed. These patterns are interrelated; collapse on one layer calls for an overcompensation by another layer.

Asthma is a good example of conflicts in pouches and layers. The lungs don't know whether to exhale or inhale. The structure either does not or cannot breathe, yet at the same time it is trying to. The chest wants to descend to help exhalation yet it cannot, so it remains elevated. The alveoli cannot contract and are held open, even though the brain screams to get air. Inhalation takes place in a rapid emergency style because the brain cannot tell the lungs to exhale. Respiration is haywire as neither inhalation nor exhalation completes itself.

Overbound and underbound layers reflect pulsatory conflict. One layer may have a functional good feeling, while another is over-aroused, a third is inhibited. We freeze, hold, wait in the skeletal muscle while the brain races to see if there is danger or not. We inhibit the muscles of action in the skeleton but become hyperactive in the viscera or vice versa. In stiffness and collapse, expansion and contraction are in conflict, unable to decide between bracing and attacking or folding in and fleeing. On one layer we remain pleasant, act social, protect our external image, while at another layer we shrink, feel despair, wish to cry out for help. We are happy on the outside, crying on the inside. Or we might be a gloomy, despairing person on the outside, and buoyant and positive inside.

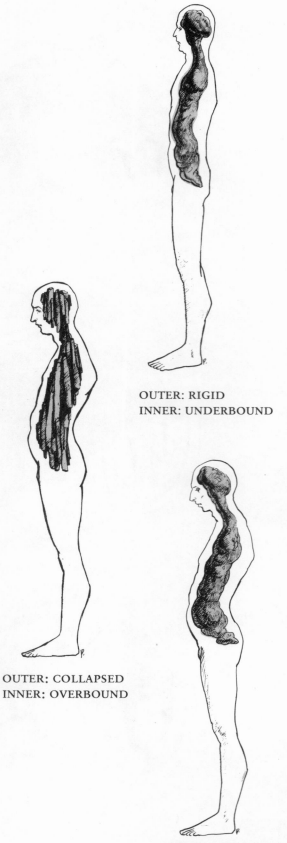

OUTER: RIGID
INNER: UNDERBOUND

OUTER: COLLAPSED
INNER: OVERBOUND

OUTER: COLLAPSED
INNER: UNDERBOUND

77 THE LAYERS OF THE STRESS PATTERN

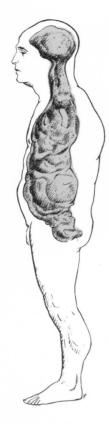

OUTER: DENSE
INNER: UNDERBOUND

OUTER: SWOLLEN
INNER: OVERBOUND

OUTER: RIGID
INNER: OVERBOUND

OUTER: DENSE
INNER: OVERBOUND

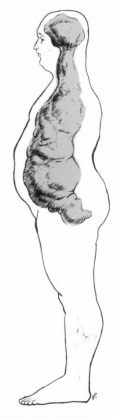

OUTER: SWOLLEN
INNER: UNDERBOUND

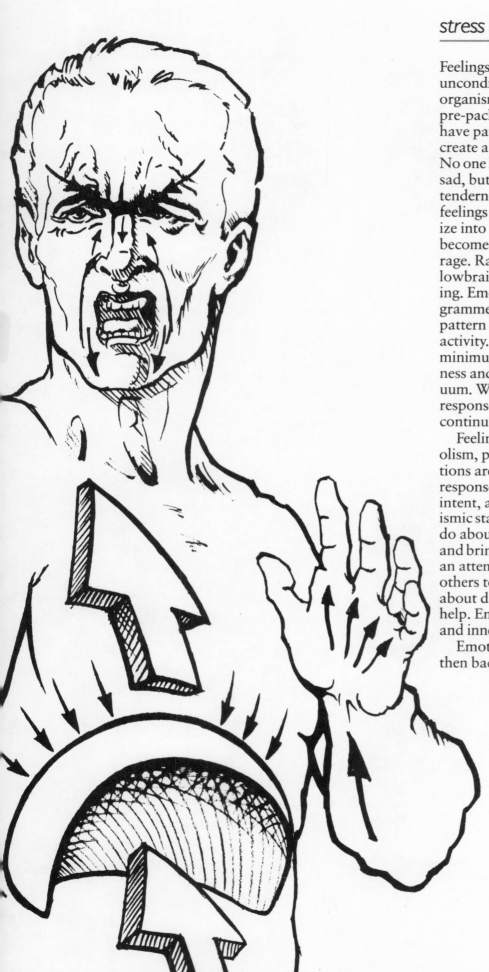

Feelings and emotions differ. Feelings are unconditioned, unprogrammed, generalized organismic states, whereas emotions are pre-packaged programs of behavior that have pathways for action. Feelings need to create a pathway in order to be expressed. No one has to teach a person to be rageful or sad, but we do have to learn kindness and tenderness. Thus, emotions are made up of feelings that have enough intensity to organize into a behavioral pattern. Annoyance becomes irritation, then anger, and finally, rage. Rage is an automatic response with a lowbrain program of striking out or attacking. Emotion is a bodily state with a programmed muscular pattern as well as a tubal pattern of speeded-up or slowed-down activity. Emotional intensity ranges from minimum to maximum. For example, sadness and grief are part of the same continuum. While the feeling is the same, the response intensifies as it continues along the continuum.

Feeling is a by-product of cellular metabolism, pulsation, and tubal peristalsis. Emotions are the organized gross behavioral responses. Emotions have direction and intent, a logic of their own. They are organismic statements about our state and what to do about it. If we are sad, crying gives relief and brings consolation from others. Anger is an attempt to get rid of an irritant and warn others to keep away. Fear is a statement about danger as well as an act of seeking help. Emotions thus seek to change outer and inner situations.

Emotions move us toward the world and then back to ourselves. When we expand toward the world we are full of ourselves. We seek either to give ourselves or to reach out and get. Alternately, we may seek to push the world away. In the contraction cycle we take in what we have received or we withdraw from the world. Emotions crest and trough, well up and recede. They follow the expansion-contraction cycle. When the continuum of emotional expression remains flexible, we go from anger to sadness, from contraction to swelling, yet always return to a homeostatic state of balanced arousal. As continuing insult distorts somatic shape, the full range of emotional expression is lost.

The startle continuum follows the principles of expansion and contraction. Swelling, inflating, shrinking, compacting are an emotional continuum. We keep people at a distance by becoming rigid and threatening, contracting and becoming dense, swelling up and becoming menacing, or collapsing and becoming unresponsive. We may try to get from the world by attacking it, withdrawing and denying our need, swelling to appear big and important, or withdrawing and hoping people will take care of us. Emotions thus are expressions of intent, the direction we follow, and the intensity that results in overbound and underbound behavior.

If we are continually promised things and then thwarted we may become angry. If this continues we become rigid, always attacking others. Anger may also create fear around acting, thus we become rigid and fearful. We may feel disgusted and contract or pull back from the world into ourselves. We may feel disparaged, non-participative, become dense, resentful, pessimistic. Our desperation to get something may cause us to swell up, to act as though we are important in order to gain acceptance. We try to get into the world to overcome our own sense of emptiness. We may become so discouraged that we collapse in fatigue or retreat into resignation and defeat. These postures become a way of organizing ourselves and a way of feeling, thinking, and acting. They are the way we tell others as well as ourselves about who we are.

Emotions are an expression of an internal environment and are related to motility and pulsation. This relationship is reciprocal. Pulsation generates emotion and feeling. Emotion and feeling influence pulsation. Pulsation is a pump function. When the pumping function is over-aroused feelings are inflamed and inflated. When the pumping function is inhibited emotional expression and feeling is diminished. Anger and rage brace and stiffen us and pulsation increases. Sadness and defeat soften and liquify us and pulsation decreases. Emotional expression is thus affected by the perpetuation of a stress pattern.

Good muscle tonus is based on a wave of tubal pulsation with a full range of expansion and contraction. The diaphragm and body wall are soft but firm, the abdomen and chest are flexible, capable of expansion and contraction. The center of gravity resides in the abdominal-pelvic basin rather than the thoracic pouch. A general feeling of well-being, a daily ease is reflected in a soft firm arousal. There is healthy plasticity. However, under continual stress, the body fixates in emergency emotions—anger, rage, fear, panic, horror, helplessness, hopelessness, despair, apathy. These emotions involve extremes of movement away from good tonus. The person moves toward either rigidity or collapse.

IMAGE SEVENTY-EIGHT. The inflation response to stress. Overboundedness, the first half of the stress continuum, involves patterns of expansion and inflation that expand us, lift us upward, make us bigger. Under stress we first rise up out of the abdomen. We inflate the chest and compress the stomach. We stiffen the neck to appear bigger, more alert. We build up kinetic potential, ready to hit. In severe situations we pull up the pelvic floor, stiffen the legs, lift the shoulders, withdraw the genitals, lock the spine tight, round the neck as if to butt, clench the mouth and hands, and brace. As we pull into the upper body, the diaphragm, normally lowered and spread wide, rises and narrows. With escalation of stress the diaphragm ascends, increasing inter-thoracic pressure, forcing the abdominal viscera upward. As we move into fear we become spastic. The diaphragm is restricted. We suffer from lack of oxygen. We have feelings of fatigue.

78 THE INFLATING EMOTIONS—PRIDE, ANGER, FEAR

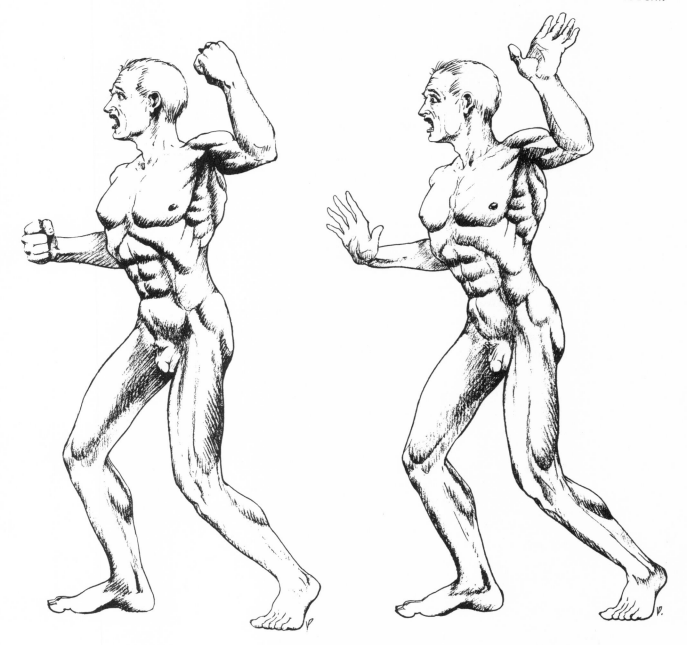

IMAGE SEVENTY-NINE. The deflation response to stress. Underboundedness, the latter half of the stress continuum, involves contraction, becoming smaller, retreating into ourselves. Descent occurs when we either have been defeated or decide to submit or collapse. The abdominal contents descend due to lack of torso muscle tone. The sag of the intestines drags the diaphragm down, and the intercostal muscles collapse. This is in sharp contrast to the spasticity of the anger-fear pattern. The muscles of the spine lose their tone, and sag deepens into a downward descent away from erectness. As descent continues into the abdominal world, the organs prolapse through the perineum. There is a curve in the neck as well as in the lumbar spine, making the chest sink in. We try to hold the head erect with occipital muscle spasms. The brain, pharynx, and heart sag downward. The rigidity of the neck keeps the air passages open. As we escalate from soft retreat into crying or intensive sobbing and helplessness, abdominal protrusion escalates, the diaphragmatic dome flattens more, the upper chest costal muscles get atrophic, the pressure of drag pulls us down, the psoas slackens as the anterior torso flexes and bends forward. There is increased density, a loss of pulsation in the brain, a loss of elasticity and rebound in the chest wall. The sternum clavicle compresses, forcing us inward. As we further descend into helplessness, the chest collapses, forcing expiration. The psoas and adductors begin to be pulled in and up to prevent collapse. The hands open in supplication. The neck shortens. We shrink and lose some of our upright stance as the spine rounds and becomes fixed with elongated and overstretched muscles.

In both these extremes there is a loss of uprightness. Stiffening is accompanied by a compression of pulsation as internal pressure increases through the muscle layers and compacted organs. In descent pulsation intensifies through downward sag and abdominal swelling. As the waves of pulsation that make for uprightness are lost, we become either rigid with rage or fear, or limp with defeat and helplessness.

Muscle tone, its firmness or weakness, determines the quality and duration of an

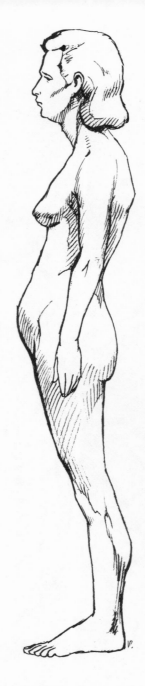

emotion. Equally, the vitality of metabolism, oxygenation, and visceral motility influences emotional expression. Emotional expression reflects the spasticities or weaknesses of the organism. Emotions depend upon interorganismic cooperation for their relief or expression. The continuous expansive stress patterns extend the organism upward and rigidify it. The emotions of assertion, pride, anger are invoked. The continuous contractive stress patterns involve a descent into collapse with the accompanying emotions of retreat, submission, defeat, and helplessness.

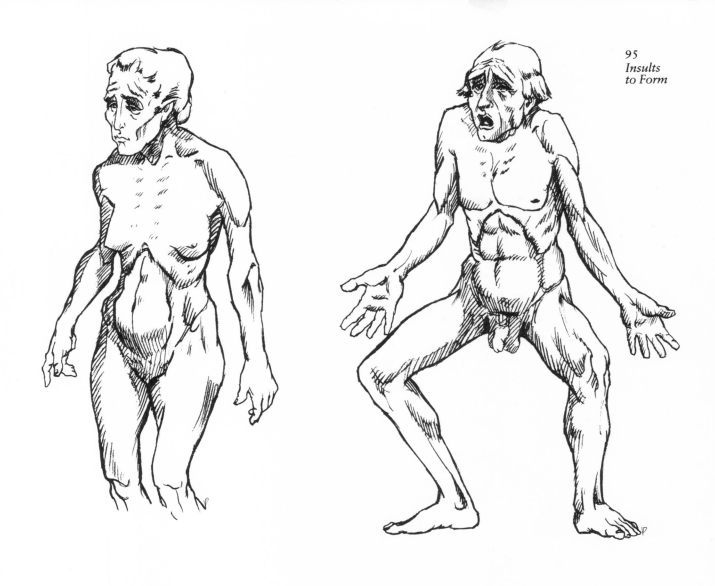

79 THE DEFLATING EMOTIONS—RETREAT,
COLLAPSE, DEFEAT

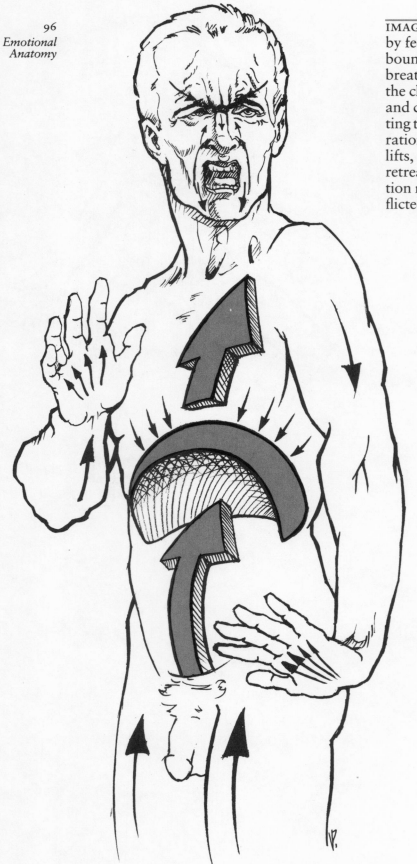

Uplifted inspiration invoked by feelings of contempt or dislike. Over-bound emotional expression distorts breathing. The diaphragm is depressed as the chest pulls up to inspire. The intestines and chest pull up as the spine extends, putting the diaphragm in conflict between expiration and inspiration. The head flexes and lifts, a dissociating gesture of olfactory retreat. The paradox of this breathing position results in a neurotic diaphragm conflicted about which direction to commit to.

IMAGE EIGHTY-ONE. Deflated expiration invoking the emotions of despair and grief. Sobbing involves rapid movements of the diaphragm. Because of the protruding belly the inspiratory motions are short, at the same time the diaphragm must make longer shortening actions to expel air in crying. The abdominal muscles act as a bellows to expel the air while the rib cage and intercostals make violent downward action. The direction of the arrows shows the diaphragm's movement and the muscle contractions that give expression to the emotion.

The emotions of anger, pride, rage, fear, sadness and grief influence and are influenced by the range of respiration. The two halves of the stress continuum distort expansion and contraction and lead to a continuous state of feeling and emotion which we know as ourselves.

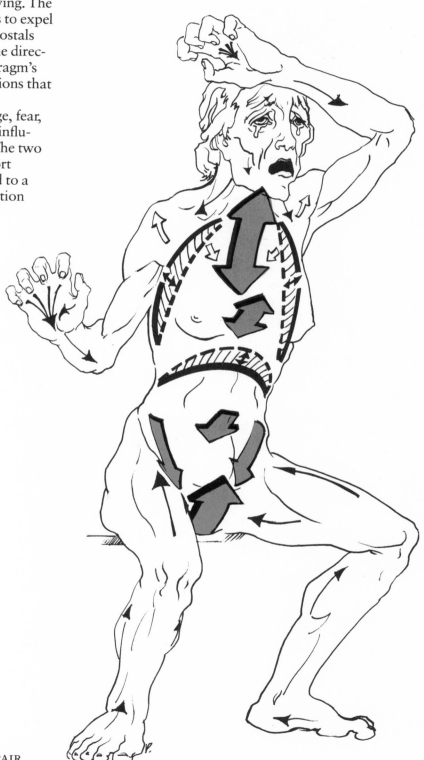

IMAGE EIGHTY-TWO. The effects of over-bound emotional patterns on various compartments and pouches. The acute expansion pattern of investigation, bluff, or annoyance permanently affects the organism. Chronic attitudes of pride, fear, or imitation strength results in an inability to lower the chest and shoulders in exhalation, giving in, or softening. The completion of expiration is not possible since the intercostals, diaphragm, neck, head, and spine muscles cannot stop pulling up in order to expel. The emotional result is anxiety, fear of being small, and the dynamics of superiority and dominance. Chronic inspiration is the stance of performance. At the same time the contraction and squeezing of the lower abdomen and pelvis compress motility.

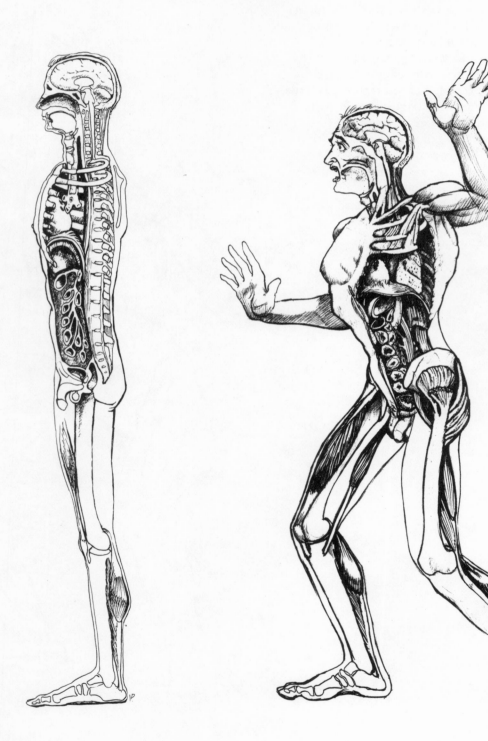

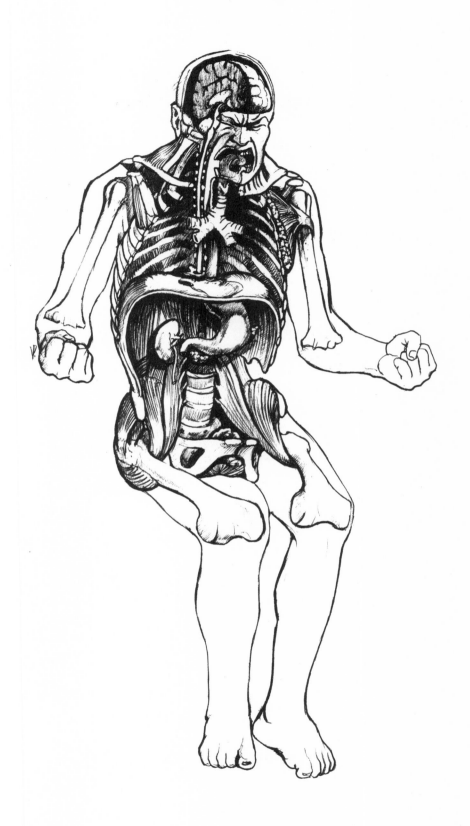

82 **THE EFFECT OF THE INFLATING
EMOTIONS ON POUCHES AND LAYERS**

IMAGE EIGHTY-THREE. The effects of under-bound emotional patterns on compartments and pouches. There is a chronic contraction pattern. Oxygenation is lowered causing inhibition of sensations in the throat, chest, and mouth. Motility in the esophagus, bronchi, nasopharynx, and lungs diminishes. The emotions of defeat, weakness, small-ness, and low self-esteem are predominant. Overbound inflation defends by exaggera-tion. Underbound deflation defends by withdrawal. Overbound people can become a menace to others; underbound people are not a menace to anyone. In chronic contrac-tion, feelings are centered in the distended viscera. The uplifted chest of the overbound exaggerates feelings of dominance while the distended abdomen of the underbound promises sexuality but, in reality, is passive.

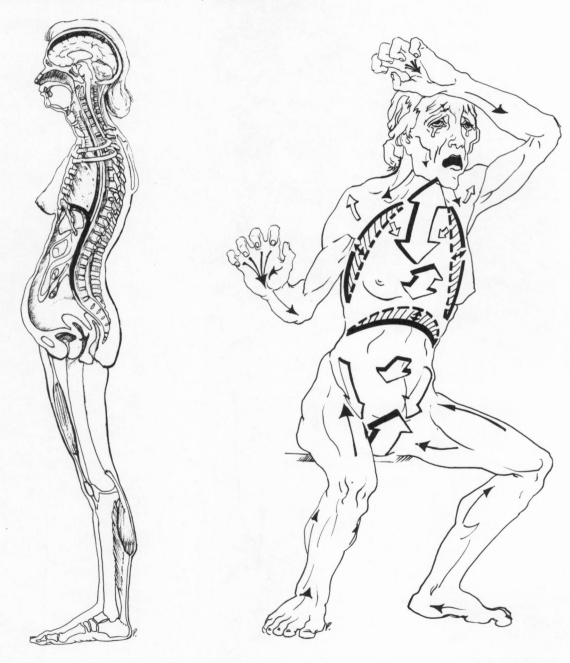

83 THE EFFECT OF THE DEFLATING
EMOTIONS ON POUCHES AND LAYERS

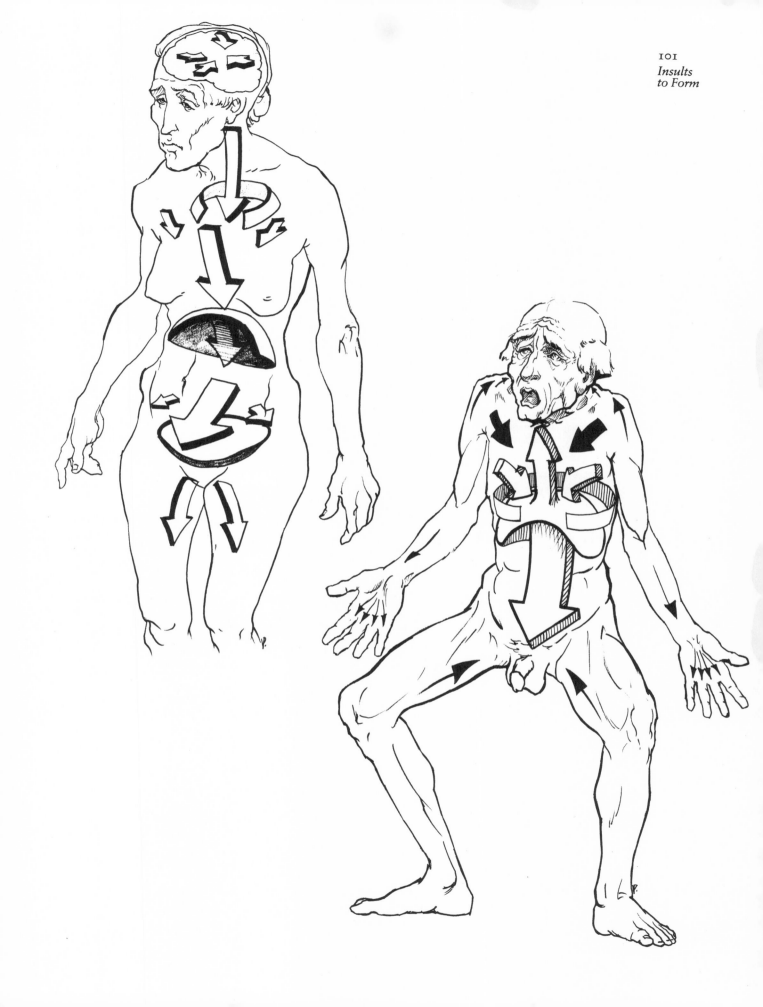

All these images demonstrate that emotions can be layered or compartmentalized. Anger may be localized in the head: the mouth, brain, and eyes bulge while powerful contractions of the neck muscles and clavicles serve to contain or localize the feeling. Or anger or sadness could be localized in the thorax, hidden from view by spasms in the bronchi, trachea, and tongue.

The ballooning of the lungs and chest wall as found in pride or anger makes breathing difficult as does its opposite, the compression of the lungs and chest wall. The abdomen can be ballooned out from inner diaphragmatic pressures, emotionally holding back the urge to expel or not give at all. It may be under control as if to show no fear. This occurs through powerful anal, buttock, and perineal tensions that keep the adductors and abductors of the legs in constant spasticity.

The compartments reflect emotional states of liveliness, irritation, deadness, or weakness. These same states are reflected in the layers. The outer skin may be red with rage or shame, flushed by the autonomic nervous system. This occurs when one is livid with terror, fear, or shock. Or it may be pale white from the draining of surface blood to the capillary lakes in the abdomen. The brain and senses may be overactive with the impulses of defense or underactive in the need to hibernate. Cold and hot dampen and arouse the outer tube of skin and nerves.

The skeletal muscles, cartilage, and bone make up the next layer where we can become rigid with the emotions of fear and anger or lose muscle strength if shocked into swelling or collapse. Muscles that are unsure and weak cannot support strong expressions of emotion. The strength of the middle layer increases in pride and defiance, diminishes with helplessness and grief.

Cathartic release, in and of itself, does not shape emotional behavior. Fixed emotional patterns are layered or compartmentalized and are based on distortions of expansion and contraction. In order to deal with the continuation of stress we make ourselves either bigger and over-aroused or smaller and under-aroused. These overbound and underbound states are accompanied by emotional patterns making us angry, rageful, and defiant or sad, grieving, and hopeless. Emotional expression is based on uprightness, the wave of tubal pulsation. Insult and stress distort that wave. The organism utilizes a continuum of responses to meet the insult. Yet each response— rigidity, density, swelling, and finally, collapse—fixates the organism in over or under arousal. Tubes, layers, pouches, and diaphragms come into play to provide the necessary response. The organism loses its full range of emotional expression and knows itself in a limited emotional range. The exaggerations of the stress pattern, stiffening and shrinking, form the basis of on-going emotional states. The expression of feeling requires more than reorganizing expansion or contraction, or softening patterns of fear and anger, utilizing muscle softening techniques. Rather a dialogue must be established among all the levels of pulsation and their emotional expressions. Muscular social patterns of coordination and speaking must be established. New emotional expressions have to be organized.

four

patterns of
somatic distress

overbound and
underbound structures

THE ASSERTIVENESS of pulsations and the circulation of excitatory currents result in the feelings, urges, and psychological states that make up our lives. Somatic shape expresses what we have experienced, our satisfactions as well as our disappointments.

How we feel is based on our ability to sustain, organize, and express excitation. When pulsatory currents are dampened, stilled, over-aroused, or concentrated, so too is the expression of feeling. Teachers understand this. In training a child to learn and concentrate they tell him to still his excitation. The military also understands this. In order to be brave and avoid fear soldiers are taught to pull their intestines in and lift and lock their chests. This dampens fear in the intestines while it excites the chest.

This chapter presents an in-depth view of the rigid, dense, swollen, and collapsed structures. The emotional organization of the four structures demonstrates how morphology expresses personal experiences and conflicts, how layers and inner tubes are affected, where conflictual contraction occurs, how motility is distorted, what happens to excitation and its currents, and what is the emotional result. The four images are presented on a progressive continuum that goes from stiffening (fixated muscular expansion) to compacting (fixated muscular contraction) to swelling (fixated pouch expansion) to finally, collapse (fixated pouch contraction). At one extreme the person gets bigger—rigid and swollen structures—while at the other end he gets smaller—the dense and collapsed types. While both rigidity and swelling are disturbances of expansion, they differ in their organization, muscles versus pouches, and their intent. Rigidity is meant to keep the other away, swelling to bring the other close. The same is true of the compaction disturbances, density and collapse. One is a muscular, the other a pouch phenomenon. Density is also meant to keep the other away, while collapse is meant to draw in the other.

Each type is presented first as a pattern of emotional expression, then as an overall gestalt, and finally in the general aspects previously developed—tubes, layers, pouches, diaphragms, excitation and motility. At the end of each typology is a visual overview and a summary table. The chapter closes with a comparison of the various emotional structures and suggestions for helping reorganize each structure.

the rigid structure

IMAGE EIGHTY-FOUR. The emotional stance of the rigid. Each type presents an emotional message to the world. The rigid type says, "I won't," "I am bigger than you," "give me recognition and appreciation." The rigid stiffens, pulls back, braces, and elongates in emotional stances of pride and challenge. The rigid person performs, dominates, and controls by assertion. He thinks caution. He is a rejecter. This type pushes the other away by introjecting him. He makes others appear small by making himself bigger. "Stay away" is the message he conveys and the response he hopes to evoke. This state is meant to deal with feelings that arise from within, feelings of loneliness, weakness, or need against which the rigid stiffens or braces. To do this he acts against his viscera, holding them in or blowing them out.

Rigidity is a survival strategy arising in families that supply the basic essentials of emotional support. Generally speaking, rigid structures have parents who did not abandon or abuse them; rather they were challenged at a later period in their development. Their stance is basically assertive.

Rigidity is a result of a familial organization that demands that the child remain fixed in specific behaviors, for example, no crying or expression of anger. It is a danger for the growing child to violate this code of behavior. He fixates in the early stages of startle, locked in to be alert, ready to push away others, his own impulses, and anything that may provoke him to be out of control. The opposite may also occur; that is, anger and attack may be taught as a way of solving conflict. The individual learns to be feisty, belligerent, intimidating, and openly aggressive rather than adopting the milder forms of stiffening or fleeing. Likewise, the person may learn that his fear brings about others' withdrawal.

The rigid family demands that the child control his pulsations. The child resists by engaging in power disputes, overactivity, resistance, and willfulness. The stance of uprightness becomes too stiff. The rigid lacks flexibility and remains on a narrow track of responses.

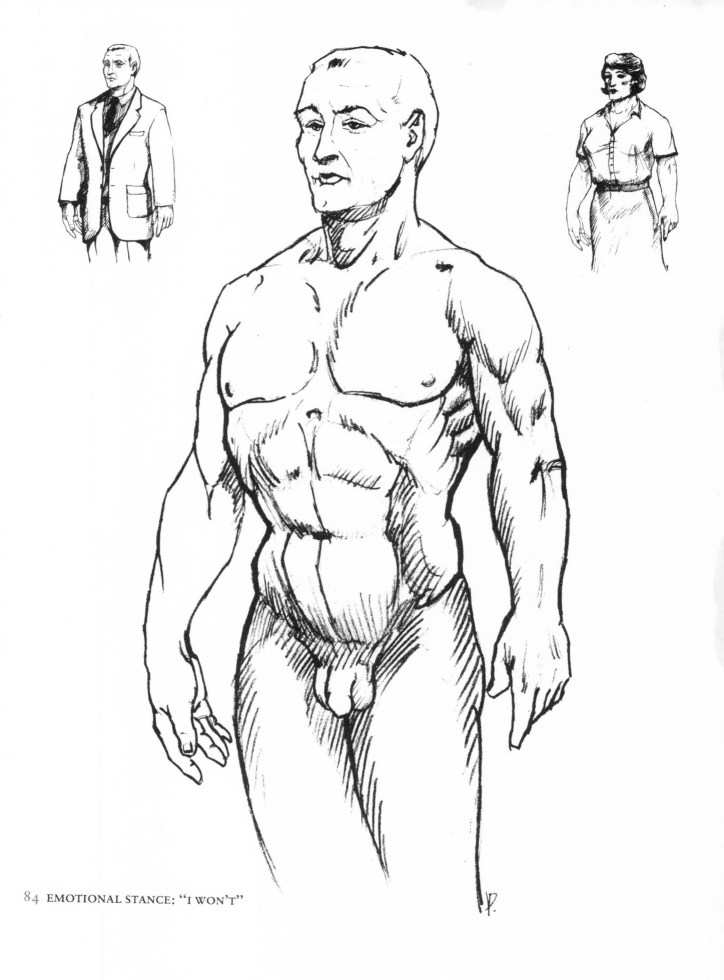

84 EMOTIONAL STANCE: "I WON'T"

IMAGE EIGHTY-FIVE. Direction of force: the rigid structure. The general stance of the rigid structure is to pull up, pull back, stiffen and brace. The head pouch swells, the brain is overactive, the head pressures outward, the chest pouch lifts, thus contracting the interior intercostals and stretching the exterior intercostals. There is lordosis in the lumbar spine. The outer extensions of the spine contract. This results in the rib cage pulling upward and backward, which spreads the lower ribs forcing the diaphragm into a conflict between the wish to descend and its upward pull. Both breathing in and breathing out are affected. The abdominal muscles contract, asserting upward diaphragmatic pressure. The internal organs pull up, inflating the chest and head.

The rigid compresses, isolates, inhibits and localizes excitation. He locks his excitation into a separate pouch to separate it from the rest of the organism. He localizes excitation in the skeletal muscles, the middle layer or support system, and the top brain. His peristalsis becomes angular and shortened, like a person with colitis. Pulsation is erratic, shallow, localized. He feels dark, solid, and non-expansive. The forces of contraction conflict with his over-expansion.

When he is viewed as a tube, different dynamics become evident. The rigid, as an upright tube, elongates. The lower pouch compresses and the upper pouches blow up. The rigid's structure is like a half-used tube of toothpaste, squeezed upwards. His peristalsis pushes upward to maintain pressure; thus, the accordion-like function of expansion and contraction becomes taut. His body appears bigger than it is in an exaggerated erectness designed to impress or frighten others. This person appears to others as explosive.

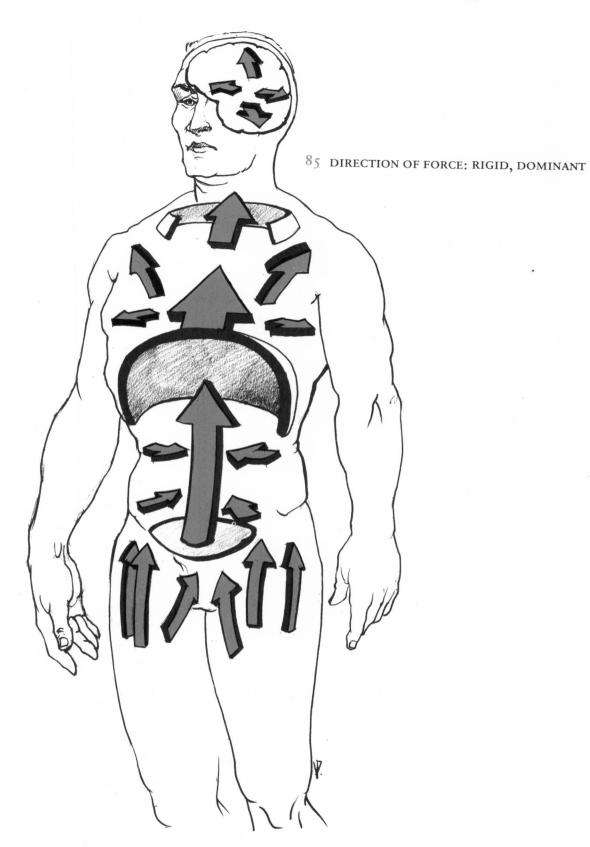

85 DIRECTION OF FORCE: RIGID, DOMINANT

IMAGE EIGHTY-SIX. A rigid tube as a body form. Tubes, layers, pouches and diaphragms sustain a vertical wave of pulsation. In resisting stress, the quality of the organism's uprightness is affected. In rigidity the tubes stiffen and become spastic. The structure is stiff, unyielding but brittle. The pelvis and spine pull back in combativeness, hyperactivity, heightened alertness. There is inflexibility with an intense focus, a hardened form with narrowed yet intense excitation. The muscular wall narrows as does the central passageway, putting the internal tubes under pressure, which makes passage of their contents difficult. There is a build-up of kinetic energy which is waiting to attack or let go and collapse. This stance is both angry and fearful. The structure is frozen in over-expansion, pulled backward and upward.

Patterns of defense involve the total organism. Being erect and sustaining the pouches is the function of muscle and bone in the field of gravity. Outer skeletal muscle, volitional-striated muscle, forms a tube that acts as a container while giving us a specific shape. It gives firmness by attaching to harder structures like bone or tendons. This permits stable scaffolding to keep us erect, resisting the forces of gravity. Muscle tone increases in strength, thickness, and endurance as we overcome the gravitational challenges to come closer to earth. The bones are levers which support action and keep muscle movement within certain channels for the greatest efficiency. So muscle and bone coordinate to give a stable, upright form with movement that is predictable and efficient. Rigid structures use their muscles to be erect. They have little sense of inner support, so they fear letting their muscles relax.

86 A RIGID TUBE AS A BODY FORM

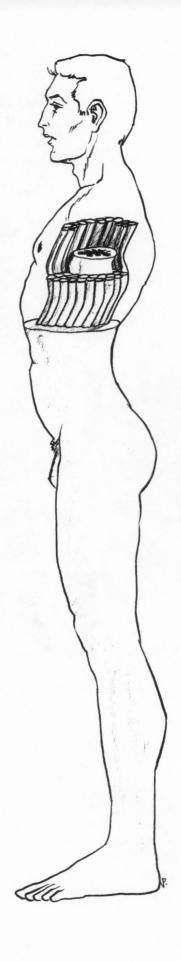

Standing is thus a complex biological, sociological, mechanical, organic, emotional event. It is a series of layers of peristaltic waves, each with its own rhythm, going from head to toe. We stand because the waves of all our tubes—digestive, respiratory, muscular, and skeletal—interact to maintain a persistent peristalsis. Stiffening in fear affects uprightness. Uprightness is based on a dynamic interplay between a series of outer and inner muscles: the long muscles of the spine, the rectus muscles of the head, the longissimus group of muscles, the rotators, the interspinal and inter-transverse muscles, the multifidus group, the quadrate muscles of the loins, the oblique muscles of the abdomen, the ham-strings, the rectus muscles of the thigh, the gastrocnemius muscles, the rectus muscles of the abdomen, the sterno-cleidomastoid muscles—and the bones of the spine, hip, legs, head.

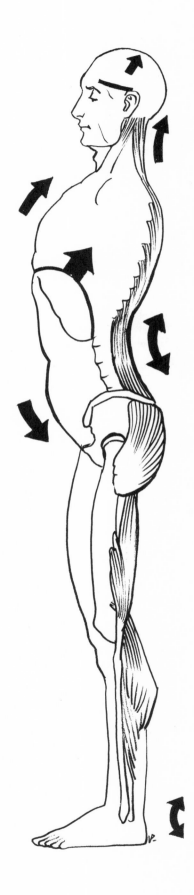

IMAGE EIGHTY-SEVEN. Rigid uprightness —pulled back. The arrows indicate that the front of the body wall extends and stretches at the same time that the muscles of the spine pull back. The lumbar and cervical curves increase; the muscles shorten. The stance pulls back yet is ready to go forward, somewhat like an arrow in a drawn bow, a readiness to attack. The person could also pull back in fear. The muscles at the base of the head shorten in the back. The chest and diaphragm pull up. There are powerful contractions in the buttocks, the quadriceps, the thighs and the calves. As the head pulls back, intercranial pressure raises. This affects the contents of the brain. It also affects the abdomen and the spine. The outer layer pulls up yet stretches apart. The rigid person is off balance. The pale muscle fibers, the slow contractors, and the inter-axial muscles dominate. They overcome the faster muscle action of the chest flexors which want to close up. The integrity of the pouches is still maintained. They are intact but amplified.

87 RIGID, PULLED BACK, WITHHOLDERS: ANTI-GRAVITY STANCE

IMAGE EIGHTY-EIGHT. Rigid uprightness —pulled-up. Here is a different organization of the anti-gravitational ring. The pelvic and thoracic pouches lose their distinctiveness, but this does not extend to the head. In order to brace against falling backward, the biceps, hamstrings, and abdominal muscles contract strongly. These contractions pull the pelvis forward and the floating ribs move down through the abdominal obliques. The chest descends. The abdominal contents are forced upward as there is conflict between expiration and a diaphragm locked to inspire. The sternocleidomastoid and scalene muscles contract to brace the head, overcoming the tendency to pull it back. The forces in the head compress and squeeze toward the center. They direct upward instead of upward and back. This changes the position of erectness to one of challenge, to hold it, to inhibition, a stance resembling the fourth position on the startle/stress continuum.

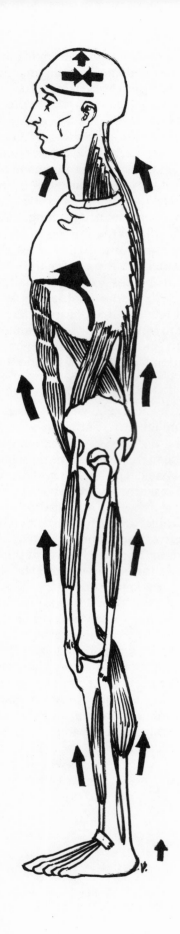

88 RIGID, PULLED UP, DOMINATORS:
ANTI-GRAVITY STANCE

IMAGE EIGHTY-NINE. Pump function: rigid, pulled-back. In this form of rigidity, the pump-function is expanded in the pelvic, thoracic, and cranial vaults. Here the diaphragm is capable of greater expansions and contractions in the downward, upward, and side-wall excursions. The arrows show the force of this vertical amplification. Contraction generates tremendous motility and pulsation rather than inhibiting it. Each chamber or pouch expands. Segmental expansion and contraction give the pump tremendous filling and emptying capacity. It is like the heart when the power of the stroke is increased. It is not that the pump beats faster but that it beats with more power and rhythmicity.

The general function of respiration, the pouch dynamics, and the feelings that these stances produce are based on the operation of the internal pumps. What happens to the pelvic-abdominal, thoracic, and cranial pump under conditions of overboundedness? Each pump forms a clear, independent structure whose integrity is important to maintain the cross-sectional layering as well as vertical expansion and contraction. A pump is made up of the interaction of a series of layers. The outer layer is a thick connective tissue layer with accompanying fascia deeply networked by nerve pathways, sense organs, and blood vessels. The second layer is made up of muscle, bone, and cartilage, followed by the third layer of inner organs and their hollows. The pump function also involves the diaphragms and the outer body wall. In coordinated pumping action there is an accordion-like function in each segment that elongates and shortens separately and together. In the pumping chambers excitation is mobilized, sustained, intensified, and transmitted to other segments.

IMAGE NINETY. Pump function: rigid, pulled-up. A stiff, pulled-up person with a rigid pump. The abdominal pelvic pump compresses and pumping narrows. The strokes between the upper and lower chambers intensify as overall pressure increases. The cranial dural space is flexible. The accordion-like action is restricted by rigidity yet it is still capable of a powerful piston-like action. Excitation builds up and has a potential for ejection and assertion. For the rigid structure, excitation is like powerful water pressure coming through a hose or narrow opening. The arrows show the direction of this force—upward and away from the ground.

For both these rigid structures the accordion-like pumping function is elongated. It gains a greater potential for expiration. In this sense, excitation gushes up, waiting to reverse itself.

90 RIGID PUMP FUNCTION: PULLED UP

IMAGE NINETY-ONE. Rigidity as a pattern of over-expansion. Dynamic forces interrupt excitatory flows, peristaltic pulsations, and organ motility. In this image black areas symbolize dense tissue, a lack of motility and excitation. White areas show excitation that is active and free-flowing. Striped areas show both excitation and constriction—an area that is both active and inactive. Finally, the arrows in each image indicate the direction of muscle pull or pressure.

In rigidity the shoulder muscles and pectoral muscles constrict to keep the arms at the side. The abdominal pelvic pouch contracts as do the diaphragm, the pelvic floor, and the iliopsoas muscles. The abdominal contents remain motile and excited. The rib cage and outer intercostals are spastic, while the inner intercostals are flexible. The lungs are motile. Pressure pulls the buttocks back and the calves down. The pubic area contracts for self-protection. As pressure is directed toward the head the brain becomes both overactive and inhibited. The head and thorax pull upward. These areas create a balance which serves both the outer and inner structure as defense and self-recognition. There is conflict in the head, throat, outer abdomen, and thoracic pouch yet little conflict in the main abdominal area. The outer, upper circumference is dense and not in conflict. There is excitement available in the arms and legs. The conflict of forces involves an upward excitatory rush while the thorax and head pull out of the pelvis and off the ground in a weak attempt to keep the body's balance. The result is excitation that cannot spread so it is purged in explosions and tantrums.

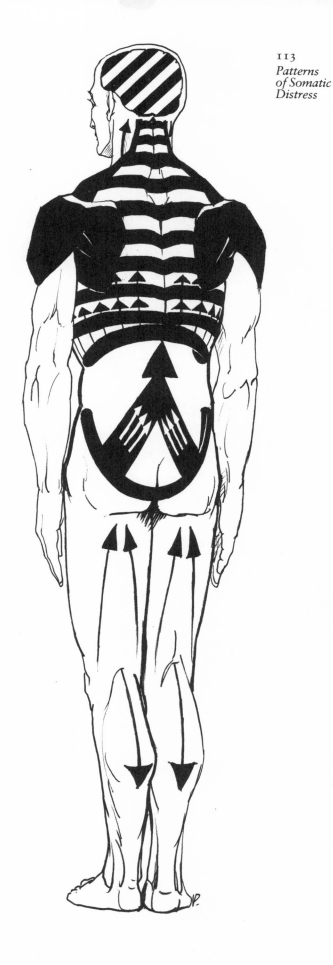

91 EXCITATORY FORCES: RIGID, OBEDIENT, CONTROLLED

somatic shape and behavioral expression

IMAGE NINETY-TWO conveys a total picture of the rigid structure and dynamics and illustrates:

- the layering principle;
- the internal and external dynamics and how they are related;

- the pouch and diaphragm principle—pouches can be pulled out of or pushed into their adjoining pouch with resulting effects on motility and peristalsis;
- the direction of forces of the total structure—out of the pelvis, off of the ground or into the pelvis, anchored to the ground;
- the configuration of the internal tubes.

Each image presents a different aspect of the structure.

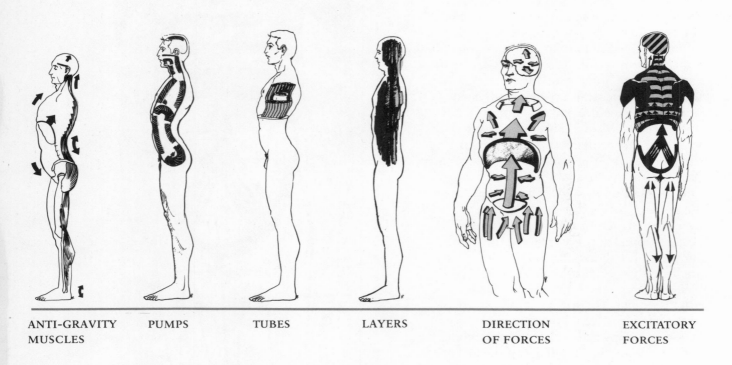

ANTI-GRAVITY MUSCLES   PUMPS   TUBES   LAYERS   DIRECTION OF FORCES   EXCITATORY FORCES

92 RIGID PATTERNS

Independence is his call,
Loneliness is his reward,
Concern is his mark,
Domination is his stamp,
Adoration is his need.
Yet scorn he gets indeed,
Arrogance is his fear,
Competence is his dream,
His secret is to be received,
To be loved, rather than to love,
He resists something coming inside him,
Yet he insists on getting inside others.

characteristics of rigid structures
the aggressive dominators
moving toward others

II5
*Patterns
of Somatic
Distress*

ROLES
Hero
Heroine
Dominator
Fighter

APPEARANCE
Pulled up
Squeezed
Frozen
Overfirm
Braced
Brittle
Aggressive

STATES OF MIND
Combat
Independence
Domination
Performance
Polarization

**FEELINGS/EMOTIONAL
QUALITIES**
Angry
Fearful
Proud
Triumphant
Attentive
Optimistic
Rageful
Reliable
Daring
Challenging
Confrontive
Generous
Cruel
Pessimistic
Sad
Explosive

FEARS
Rejection
Attack
Being small
Abuse
Dependency
Being overwhelmed
Being out of control

**TRADITIONAL
PSYCHOLOGICAL
CATEGORIES**
Phallics
Hysterics
Depressives
Manics
Projectors

**PSYCHOLOGICAL
FUNCTIONING**
Obsessive-Meticulous
Authoritative-
    Authoritarian
Inspiring-Blaming
Objectifying-
    Projecting
Optimistic-Pessimistic
Self-Righteous
Power Hungry

EXCITATION
Strong
Localized
Depressed
Agitated
Muted

MOTILITY
Persistant
Penetrating
Inhibited
Hard
Narrowed
Unabled to soften
Unable to melt

**RELATIONSHIP TO
GROUND**
Raised up
Inflexible

POUCHES
Pulled up
Pulled back
Elongated
Braced

EXPERIENCES SELF
In middle, outer layers
    of muscle, bone
In central nervous
    system
In head, shoulders,
    spine, thorax, arms,
    hands

BODY STANCE
Overactive brain
Elongated neck
Hot chest
Raised intercostals
Raised, taut
    diaphragm
Inside taut
Pulled up legs,
    illiopsoas, genitals

**BASIC
CHARACTERISTIC**
Power

RELATES TO OTHERS
Makes self bigger
Other smaller

FIGHT STYLE
Aggressive
Solitary

**AUTHORITY
RELATIONSHIP**
Dominates
Competes
Is loyal to superiors
"I'll tell you what to
    do."

AT WORK
Restrained
Conservative
Overactive
Wants control
Goes to the world
Challenging
Ritualistic
Assertive

**PEER, SUBORDINATE
RELATIONSHIP**
Dominates
Challenges
Controls
Polarizes
Is insensitive
Competes

**RELATES TO SPOUSE,
CHILDREN**
Patriarch
Matriarch

SEXUAL FUNCTIONING
Pelvis moves with
    aggression, lacks
    tenderness

**SOMATIC EDUCATION
AND CLINICAL
DIRECTION**
Destructure
Shorten
Unbrace them
Teach their outsides
    to give in, elongate,
    reach out
Challenge their
    actions
Encourage rhythmic
    soft waves
Bring them down to
    earth
Restore pulsation to
    lower pouches
Help them yield
Help soften

the dense structure

IMAGE NINETY-THREE. The emotional stance of the dense structure. The dense person says "make me," "don't humiliate me," or "I can't." Structurally he is compacted and pulled in, a statement of stubbornness and daring. Pulsation is aborted. Peristalsis is short, curtailed, seeking release from pressure. The dense structure is like a squeezed accordion. The dense type pushes away by projection onto others. He makes himself smaller by pulling in, holding in, holding down, not acting. In appearing smaller he protects himself from himself. He appears to be impotent. His feelings are based on holding on or pushing down. The dense person is caught between resisting dependency and being cautious about total independence.

The dense structure is based upon early experiences of support and expectations based upon past performance followed by disappointment and dearth of support. Both the rigid and dense structures represent early stages of startle where the organism stiffens and braces. The rigid over-expands to push the other away while the dense over-contracts to do the same thing. Both occur in the early stages of childhood where stiffening becomes a defense against fear and abandonment. The dense response comes about because of invasion. In the beginning this structure is given love. Later, when independence begins to develop, it is treated with shame and humiliation. The result is pulling back.

The dynamics of the dense family involve encouragement followed by disapproval. This results in the stiffening reflex of bracing to ward off attack. The individual accomplishes this by pulling back and compacting, pulling in and thickening the outer layers. This pattern of support, encouragement, and disapproval and the response of withdrawal compresses uprightness, obliterates the ability to elongate, pressures the internal spaces, localizes and focuses excitation in the deep organs while removing it from the surface. It is a form of hibernation—cold on the outside, hot on the inside. Tenderness is protected while aggression is turned against the self. In order to be aggressive and assertive, dense people have to squeeze or erupt. They have trouble giving. Their inclination is to withhold. There is conflict between expansion and disapproval. Taking is less hard even though they fear humiliation. They take in but hold onto. They keep their feelings close.

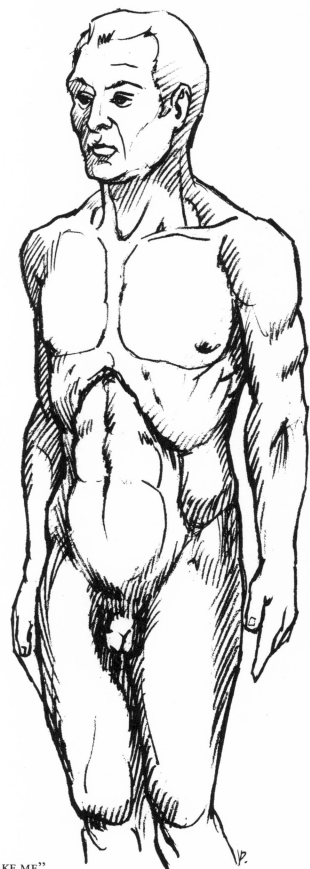

93 EMOTIONAL STANCE: "MAKE ME"

IMAGE NINETY-FOUR. Direction of force: the dense structure. The dense structure compresses, compacts, shortens but does not deflate. The internal forces compress from front to back as well as from head to pelvis. There are belts of constriction in the head, clavicles, lower ribs, and pubic circle. This downward pressure of the inner organs is facilitated by a belt around the crest of the ilium. The diaphragm fixates in the expiratory position. The pouches compress, squeeze, thicken. Thus, their inner spaces become smaller and dense. The thoracic and abdominal pouches begin to act as one. The spincter around the clavicles constricts, making the person feel strangled. Likewise the pelvis constricts with the feeling of no exit. The dense person can neither push out nor pull in. The forces all turn against each other. The brain compresses, the throat and digestive organs push down, the chest and diaphragm push down and pull in as if they were tightened by a belt. The diaphragm also pulls backward while the inner organs, the colon, prostate, and rectum, push down and inward. The anus, genitals, and buttocks push up and pull in as if they were another tightening belt. Both the adductor and abductor muscles shorten and fatten, compaction is the result. Motility is bottled up. The structure bulges.

Viewing the dense structure as a tube, different dynamics are presented. The dense structure is like an unopened tube of toothpaste that is squeezed at both the top and bottom. It will either burst or erupt like a broken dam. This is caused by the merging of the chest and abdominal pouches and the compression in the neck and around the anus. The body wall is taut, thickened, shortened. The entire tube pushes in so that the neck and waist disappear.

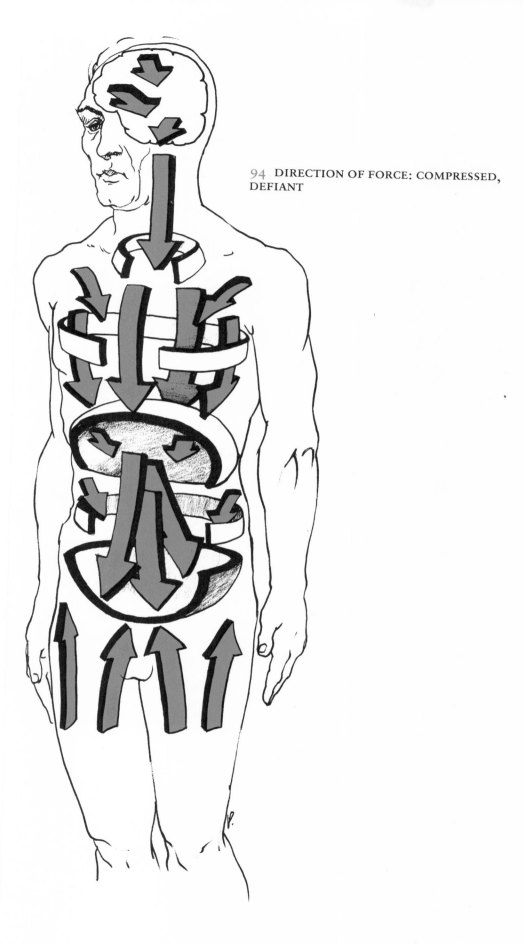

94 DIRECTION OF FORCE: COMPRESSED, DEFIANT

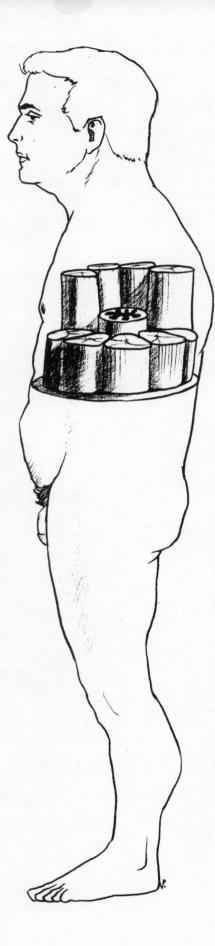

IMAGE NINETY-FIVE. The dense tube as a body form. Tubes, layers, pouches, and diaphragms sustain the vertical wave of pulsation. In resisting stress the quality of the organism's uprightness is affected. In dense structures the tubes thicken and the center of gravity is lowered. Bracing results. As the muscle fibers thicken, the inside spaces narrow. Compaction increases, passage becomes difficult. An increase of pressure is perceived as strength rather than pain. Tissue becomes dense, tightly packed, as if it were filled with glue and pressed together. This structure is based on stubbornness and defiance. Stress is met by becoming unmoved and immovable.

95 A DENSE TUBE AS A BODY FORM

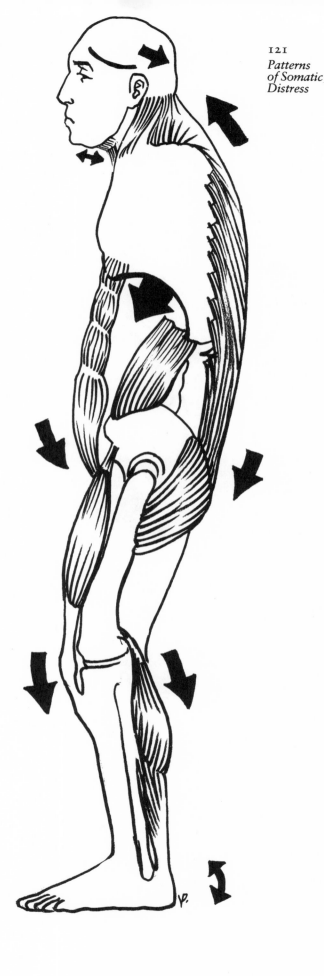

IMAGE NINETY-SIX. Dense uprightness and the anti-gravitational muscles. The head, emerging from the neck, is identified with erectness. It takes a coordinated effort to balance the head, look around, stick one's neck out. Pulling the neck in to protect the head makes it difficult for a person to maintain balance. This stance makes the person cautious. The dense person hunkers down, shortens himself, pulls his head in to prevent giving in. The outer layer becomes hypertrophic, densely packed, overused, shortened. The muscle tube becomes a fortress. The psoas and buttocks muscles contract tightly. The entire surface layer of the spinal muscles overstretches while the flexor or red fiber muscles of the front of the body tighten. The muscles of the chest wall, the neck, and the scalenes deeply contract. The occipital and neck muscles pull the head back. If they did not, the head would drop on the chest; the person would lose his balance or fold into a ball. The muscles at the front of the thigh overstretch while the calf muscles swell. The anterior obliques and the lumbar quadricep muscles shorten. The tube becomes one, like a child without a neck. The dense person is closed at the neck and throat as well as in the anal and genital sphincters. Nothing gets in or out. This creates tension. The brain is forced back and downward, its contents under pressure. The abdominal contents shove upward as the diaphragm is pushed into descent by the rib cage. Expiration is forced and shallow; inspiration becomes difficult.

96 ANTI-GRAVITY STANCE: DENSE, PULLED DOWN, DEFIANT

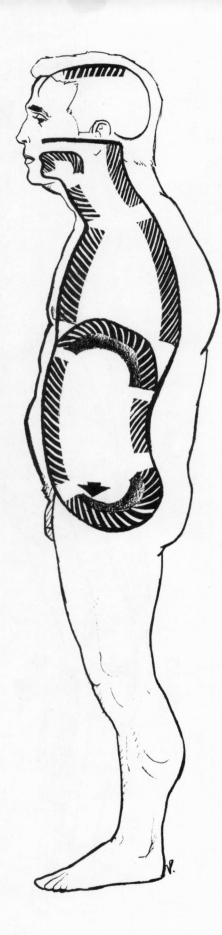

IMAGE NINETY-SEVEN. The pumping function in dense structures. Each pouch compacts and thickens and loses its ability to elongate. The dense structure feels its pouches as small yet packed. The excursion of the body wall is restricted by its thickening. The cranial pouch shortens. The abdominal and pelvic pouches merge. The arrows point to these downward and inward dynamics. Normal expansion becomes difficult. The core organs are inhibited, packed, squeezed against each other. Organs cannot pulsate freely. The accordion-like effect is that of a tight coil of gigantic power, a hydraulic press—slow, determined, steady —but not excitable. The structure is capable of withstanding great pressure until it erupts or springs a leak. Activity intensifies yet expansion or further compression is impossible. The build-up of pressure becomes the basic feeling of aliveness. The dense person controls excitation by deadening it. He localizes his excitation in the middle layers, viscera, brain stem, and mid-brain. The intense neurological excitation congeals until it erupts. Defiance, fear, and distance are the emotional statements of the dense structure.

97 DENSE PUMP FUNCTION: COMPRESSED

IMAGE NINETY-EIGHT. Density as a pattern of over-contraction. Dynamic forces interrupt excitatory flows, peristaltic pulsations, and organ motility. In this image black areas symbolize dense tissue, a lack of motility and excitation. White areas show excitation that is free-flowing. Striped areas show both excitation and constriction—areas that are both active and inactive. Finally, the arrows in the image indicate the direction of muscle pull or pressure.

In the dense or compacted structure the organization of defiance shortens the entire organism. There is heavy density in the pelvic floor, the shoulders, the brain and head vault, the surface of the body, the clavicles, shoulders, thighs, and front of the body. The arrows indicate excitation at the center but the outer layers are dense and compacted. The conflict between outer deadening and inner aliveness creates a volcanic effect, a compacted brain with a core of fire at the brain stem. Powerful forces flex the body forward in an attempt to close it, yet there is a powerful inner excitation at the core of the person.

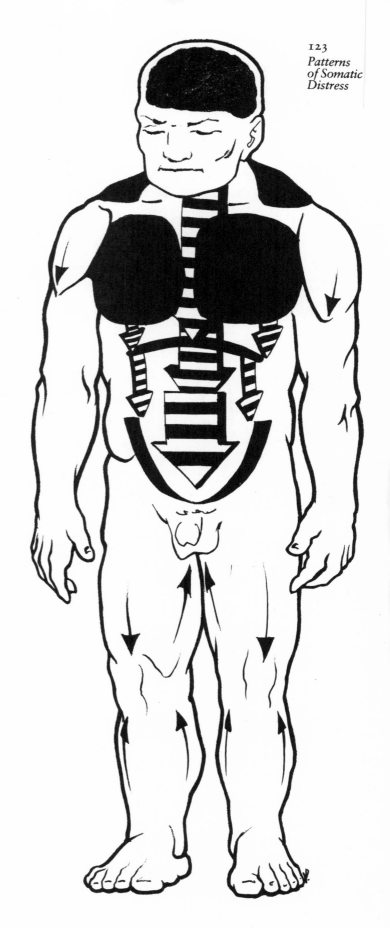

somatic shape and behavioral expression

IMAGE NINETY-NINE conveys a picture of the dense structure and dynamics and illustrates:

- the layering principle;
- the internal and external dynamics and how they are related;
- the pouch and diaphragm principle—pouches can be pulled out of or pushed into their adjoining pouch with resulting effects on motility and peristalsis;
- the direction of forces of the total structure—out of the pelvis, off of the ground or into the pelvis, anchored to the ground;
- the configuration of the internal tubes.

Each image presents a different aspect of the structure.

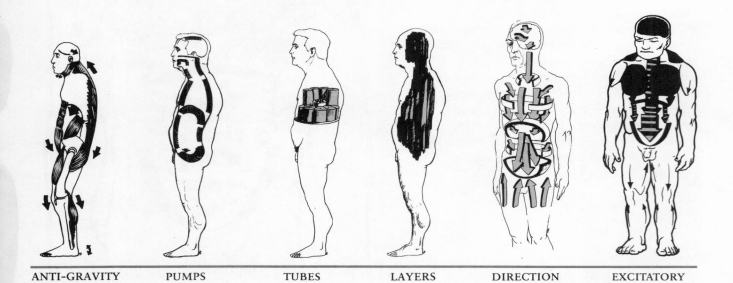

| ANTI-GRAVITY MUSCLES | PUMPS | TUBES | LAYERS | DIRECTION OF FORCES | EXCITATORY FORCES |

99   DENSE PATTERNS

Freedom is his call, martyrdom his reward.
Empathy is his mark, betrayal his fear.
Appreciation and approval are his need,
To acquire he struggles indeed.
Independence is his dream, to be at peace his desire.
His secret is to be at one with another, yet individual.
To be rooted, to belong, to be accepted without isolation.

characteristics of dense structures
the self-effacers
moving into one's self

125
*Patterns
of Somatic
Distress*

ROLES
Resister
Defender
Struggler

APPEARANCE
Compacted
Pushed down
Stuffed
Over-firm
Pressurized

STATES OF MIND
Rebellion
Struggle
Defense
Warding Off
Rejection

**FEELINGS/EMOTIONAL
QUALITIES**
Suspicious
Doubtful
Possessive
Self-effacing
Reliable
Fearful
Defeated
Hopeful
Compassionate
Defiant
Spiteful
Loyal
Servile
Determined
Stubborn
Humiliated
Empathetic
Protective

FEARS
Attacking others
Getting bigger
Independence
Attachment
Being out of control

**TRADITIONAL
PSYCHOLOGICAL
CATEGORIES**
Depressive
Passive-aggressive
Implosive
Self-denying

**PSYCHOLOGICAL
FUNCTIONING**
Pessimism versus
  reality
Denial versus
  affirmation
Independence versus
  dependence
Holding on; not
  giving up

EXCITATION
Bound outside
Internally volcanic
Eruptive
Intense
Deadened

MOTILITY
Compacted thrusts
Thick boundaries
Intense expansions
Can't melt

**RELATIONSHIP TO
GROUND**
Pushed into
Unyielding

POUCHES
Inflamed through
  compression

EXPERIENCES SELF
In skeletal muscles,
  deep intestines
In autonomic nervous
  system
In abdomen, chest,
  neck, pelvis, and
  legs

BODY STANCE
Dense brain
Shortened neck
Cool, weak chest
Lifted shoulders
Stiffened, flattened
  diaphragm
Compacted pelvis,
  legs

**BASIC
CHARACTERISTICS**
Seriousness
Withholding

RELATES TO OTHERS
Makes self smaller
Keeps others away

FIGHT STYLE
Becomes immovable
Wait it out

**AUTHORITY
RELATIONSHIP**
Seeks approval
Undermines
Is servile
"Tell me what to do"

AT WORK
Inhibited
Dedicated
Belligerent
Distrustful
Second in command
Cooperative
Cautious
Rebellious
Isolated
Assertive
Stays to self

**PEER, SUBORDINATE
RELATIONSHIP**
You come to me
Cooperative
Loyal
Indirect
Dependable

**RELATES TO SPOUSE,
CHILDREN**
Empathetic
Self-sacrificing

SEXUAL FUNCTIONING
Pelvis pushes
Sexual movement is
  squeezed
Has feeling but it is
  trapped

**SOMATIC EDUCATION
AND CLINICAL
DIRECTION**
Soften outer wall
Elongate neck from
  torso
Separate pouches
Encourage assertions
Lengthen, elongate,
  decompress
Restore rhythmicity
Move excitation and
  pulsation outwards

the swollen structure

IMAGE ONE HUNDRED. The emotional stance of the swollen structure. The emotional statement of the swollen person is "take me," "let me get to you," "give me your structure," or "give me room." This structure is blown out and eruptive. He blows up, gets bigger, intimidates, or tries to get rid of. He swells with anger yet needs to keep away from his internal contempt. Arrogance is his emotional stance. He begs for boundaries and resistance even though he seems to resist them. His real statement is "push me back so that I have a boundary." His real fear is that he will collapse.

This structure cannot move freely because either the assault he experienced occurred too early or his later moves toward independence were undermined. This occurs in families that are overprotective, manipulative, seductive, always doing things for the child and never letting him meet challenges. Alternately, the family may undermine the child, demanding that he live up to his parent's expectations. The child, in turn, screams to be let alone yet not abandoned.

The swollen structure inflates to get away from an internal build-up of needs or excitation. His peristalsis is lethargic without detectable waves yet under great pressure, like an aneurism that is capable of eruption. He tries to release the pressure or keep demands from entering in. This structure fears collapse so he distends his tubes and pumps up in an effort to keep erect. All his excitation is kept at the surface, away from the inner tubes.

The swollen person is an adultified child, a person who is thought of as an adult yet who retains many immature characteristics. This structure is preoccupied with being what others want. He gives himself in an attempt to get filled up. He has trouble withholding. He throws himself away because he lacks the ability to contain things.

In groups, in the family, at work, the swollen person is a good imitator. He identifies with others. He has insight into the needs of others and the way they function. While searching for his own identity he knows well how others function. The swollen person can be creative and giving of himself in his endeavor for an inner structural identity.

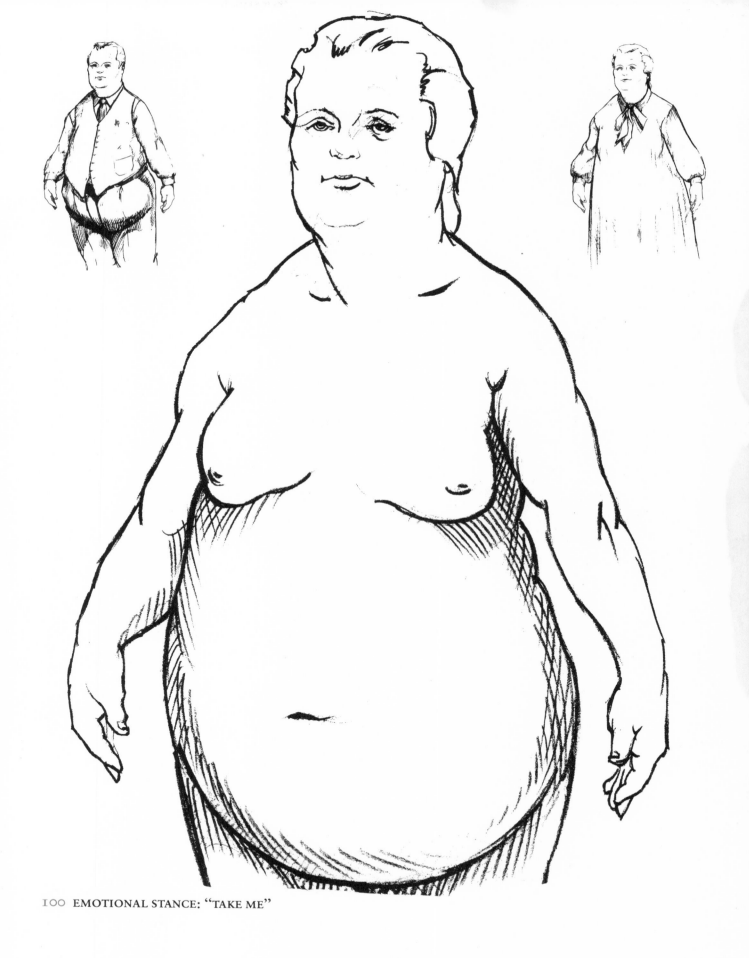

100 EMOTIONAL STANCE: "TAKE ME"

IMAGE ONE HUNDRED AND ONE. Direction of force: the swollen structure. The swollen structure over-expands, inflates, blows up like a balloon ready to burst. The expansive forces press outward. The walls thin. There is force downward and outward as pressure escalates from the inside out. All the muscles of the container thin out. The brain swells. The forces of the neck and clavicle create a suffocation-like experience. Their internal pressure narrows the chest. In the thoracic pouch, the lower ribs, abdomen, and diaphragm force outward and downward, swelling the abdomen. The pelvic and lumbar spine push forward, the pelvic diaphragm is forced down, and the pubic area forced out. The pear shape of the structure forces the adductor muscles to spread out. Peristalsis becomes minimal. The swollen structure is like the delta at the mouth of a river, spreading out, with little containment, fulminating into the environment. The excessive pouching of the abdomen creates narrowing in the chest, head, neck, and pelvic areas.

Viewed as a tube, the swollen structure displays a liquid-filled environment, one end is under pressure, the other end without contraction. The contents ooze out of one end while the other end squeezes. The abdominal pouch is over-expanded somewhat like the over-expansion of the chest pouch of the rigid. But the swollen abdomen is based on liquids and air, not muscular expansion. The tube is pouched from the inside out. The tube over-inflates with only the bones of the shoulders, head and pelvic pouch restraining further expansion. The natural contours of the body are lost. The integrity of pouches and diaphragms becomes distorted.

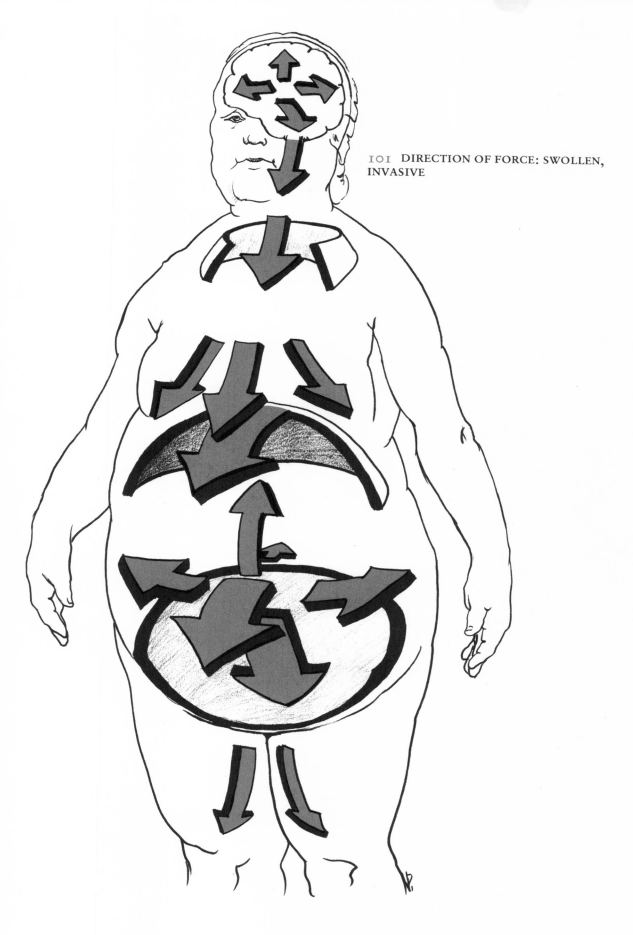

IOI DIRECTION OF FORCE: SWOLLEN, INVASIVE

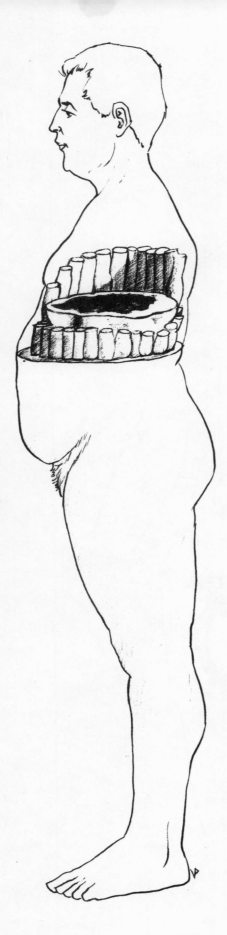

IMAGE ONE HUNDRED AND TWO. The swollen tube as a total body form. In the swollen structure the muscle wall thins and fails to provide resistance. The internal tubes inflate, expanding the pouches, which act as support. Swollen tissue is bloated; thus, it expands weakly. It swells out to take the form of the environment, inflating to become bigger. The middle layer is soft, unlike overbound forms. The swollen structure can neither move nor resist. It has difficulty containing its contents locally or generally. Things are let out but nothing gets in. This stance is invasive.

102 A SWOLLEN TUBE AS A BODY FORM

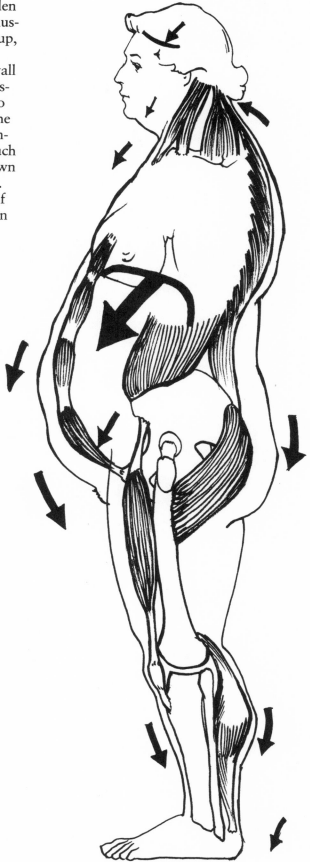

IMAGE ONE HUNDRED AND THREE. Swollen uprightness and the anti-gravitational muscles. The swollen person inflates, blows up, overexpands to keep others away. The arrows indicate that the anterior body wall in the abdomen is stretched while the posterior muscles become spastic in trying to support the body from falling over. All the weight of the upper body collapses downward. The pelvis does not pull back as much as it caves in. The diaphragm is pulled down by the weight of the abdominal contents. There is muscle contraction at the base of the neck and the calves to keep the person erect.

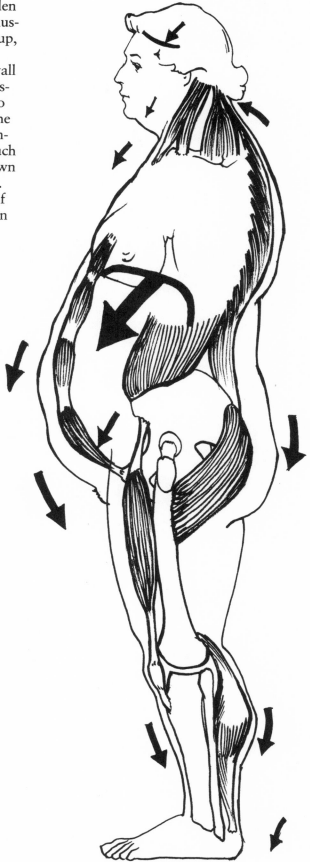

103 ANTI-GRAVITY STANCE: SWOLLEN, PUFFED UP, INVASIVE

IMAGE ONE HUNDRED AND FOUR. Pump function: the swollen structure. The swollen person relieves pressure build-up by continually expanding to the surface. His pouches feel big but empty. The pouches inflate with air, liquid, and fat, like a blowfish out of water. The result is that excitation is placed outside of himself, projected to the surface, or deadened. The swollen person moves his excitation to the surface, to his pouches, and to his top brain. Excitation serves to attract others or enables him to get into others.

The swollen person is inflated off of the ground. His chambers are thin-walled from being stretched or pulled apart. His diaphragm is flattened out to its limit, unable to recoil or come back. He can pump up, but not down. He has short, weak respiratory movements. The same is true of the exchange of liquids, gases, even emotions. He does not want others to be close. The accordion-like movement is limited, that is, he expands and contracts vertically, but very little horizontally. Swollen structures leak into the environment, they ooze, fly apart, rupture. Inner space is expanded. Organ motility is spread out rather than contained, thus, it is sluggish and unresponsive. Excitation does not carry from one pouch to another. Pumping occurs at the surface, but the body wall is thin, thus, the person is held off the ground like an inflated balloon. He feels boneless so he inflates to provide support, but this incurs the danger of becoming too spread out.

104 SWOLLEN PUMP FUNCTION: BALLOONED

IMAGE ONE HUNDRED AND FIVE. Swollenness as a pattern of over-expansion. Dynamic forces interrupt excitatory flows, peristaltic pulsations, and organ motility. In this image black areas symbolize dense tissue, a lack of motility and excitation. White areas show excitation that is active and free-flowing. Striped areas show both excitation and constriction—areas that are both active and inactive. Finally, the arrows in the image indicate the direction of muscle pull or pressure.

The swollen structure contracts his head in order to stay on the ground, not be out of control or flooded with the sensations of self or reality. The rest of the organism is over-expanded. The striped areas indicate excitation at the surface of the body, the face, throat, and core visceral organs; but there is a mild lack of excitation in the chest. The inner tube is overly motile. The stripes in the outer chest and abdomen indicate a collapsed inner function, blown-up inflatedness, and a strong attempt not to lose himself to the environment. There is conflict in the outer tube which is contracted at the top so that the inner tube can be contained.

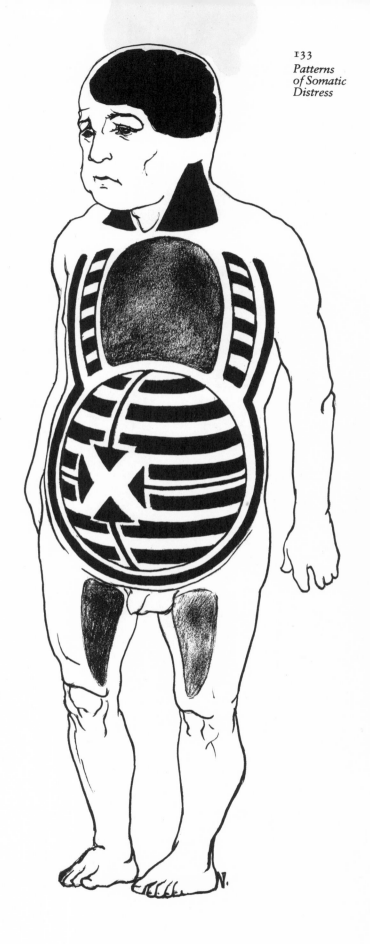

105 EXCITATORY FORCES: SWOLLEN,
MERGING, MANIPULATIVE

somatic shape and behavioral expression

IMAGE ONE HUNDRED AND SIX conveys a total picture of the swollen structure and dynamics and illustrates:

- the layering principle;
- the internal and external dynamics and how they are related;

- the pouch and diaphragm principle—pouches can be pulled out of or pushed into adjoining pouches with resulting effects on motility and peristalsis;
- the direction of forces of the total structure—out of the pelvis, off of the ground or into the pelvis, anchored to the ground;
- the configuration of the internal tubes.

Each image presents a different aspect of the structure.

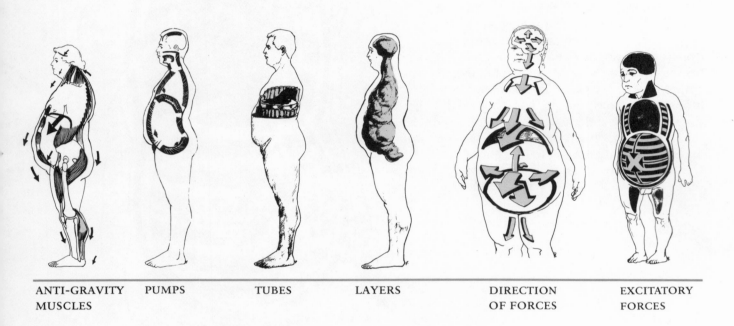

ANTI-GRAVITY   PUMPS   TUBES   LAYERS   DIRECTION   EXCITATORY
MUSCLES   OF FORCES   FORCES

106 SWOLLEN PATTERNS

Seeking a body to be in, anyone else's but their own.
All potential according to what the other wishes.
Fails to deliver even as he increases his promises.
Caught between impressing others or possessing them.
Eternally optimistic and youthful.
Always wanting to be big, yet denying his childishness.
He reside out there, engulfing or being engulfed.

characteristics of swollen structures
the inflated identifiers
move into others

135

*Patterns
of Somatic
Distress*

ROLES
Chameleon
Pretender
All things to all people

APPEARANCE
Puffed out
Inflated
Pear-shaped
Like jello

STATES OF MIND
Manipulative
Incorporative
Pretentious
Invasive
Appropriative
Tends to take over

FEELINGS/EMOTIONAL
QUALITIES
Grandiose
Dissatisfied
Self-absorbed
Narcissistic
Seductive
Identifies with others
Makes social
    excitement
Sees the possible, tries
    to join
Exploitive
Inferior
Inflamed
Sympathetic
Futurizing

FEARS
Being small
Being empty
Lack of belonging
Being incorporated

TRADITIONAL
PSYCHOLOGICAL
CATEGORIES
Manic-depressive
Narcissistic
Impulse-ridden
Grandiose
Addictive personality

PSYCHOLOGICAL
FUNCTIONING
Adultified child
Denies own needs
Makes you feel you
    need him but, in
    fact, he needs you
Superficiality

EXCITATION
Motile
Porous
Inflated
Chaotic
Inflamed

MOTILITY
Free-flowing
Lacking boundaries
Meandering
Invasive
Unable to contain

RELATIONSHIP TO
GROUND
Floats off
Resides in others

POUCHES
Exaggerated by
    swelling, inflation

EXPERIENCES SELF
In outer layers, skin,
    nerves, senses
In cortex
In hands, mouth,
    senses

BODY STANCE
Inflated head
Retreated, braced
    chest
No shoulders
Protruding diaphragm
Protruding abdomen
Wobbly legs
Living on the surface

BASIC
CHARACTERISTICS
Manipulation
Exploitation
Invasiveness

RELATES TO OTHERS
Uses others to make
    self more real,
    emotionally
    embodied

FIGHT STYLE
Mimics
Deceives

AUTHORITY
RELATIONSHIP
Political
Exploitive
Appears submissive
"I'll be what you want
    if"

AT WORK
Sociable
Ambitious
Dependable
Hard to pin down
Failing to deliver on
    promises
Seeking to take in
Talkative
Expansive
Giving of self

PEER, SUBORDINATE
RELATIONSHIP
Socializes
Demands contact
Recognizes others
Calls attention to self

RELATES TO SPOUSE,
CHILDREN
Distant
Effusive
Warm yet without
    contact
Uses for own needs

SEXUAL FUNCTIONING
Needs to be aroused
    by other
Movements are over-
    exaggerated
Can't contain feelings,
    movements

SOMATIC EDUCATION
AND CLINICAL
DIRECTION
Deflate
Compress
Teach assertion
Outside in
Challenge their
    illusions
Organize boundaries
    using body wall
Increase inner
    pressure to make
    right size
Encourage inner
    excitation and
    containment
Give structure by
    firming and
    filling in

IMAGE ONE HUNDRED AND SEVEN. The emotional stance of the collapsed structure. The emotional statements of the collapsed structure are "I can't," "give me support," or "I will take you in." He yields, shrinks, cries. He deals with fear, anger, need, or weakness by giving in. This type asks for more structure. He needs a backbone. Because he lacks a container he is dependent on others to provide it for him, in return he gives loyalty.

The collapsed person's uprightness is marginal. His gender and excitation have shrunken. He lacks commitment to the outer world or others. He can take from others if it is offered but makes little effort to get. Neither does he make much effort to give. He responds to stress by retreat and detachment. Not acting is his form of aggression. In love-making he is passive and requires excessive stimulation.

The collapsed structure comes from a family that withholds or has little excitation to give. There is deprivation of emotional nourishment. The tubal structure is given little support. This could also occur because of dietary lack, poverty, or genetic disturbances. The characteristic stance is "what's the use," so he looks to be rescued. His excitation is low but he has a deep inner fire. He has gathered his excitatory pools deep inside in a private place.

At work, in a family or a group, the collapsed person gravitates to the periphery. He is an outsider, and fades into the background. He relishes privacy as much as support. He avoids demands, but, if not discouraged, can pursue a goal with languid, persistant, and determined fortitude. At the same time he is a concerned companion, perceptive and sympathetic, with keen insight. While he does not act aggressively, he is capable of sharing in tender, gentle contact.

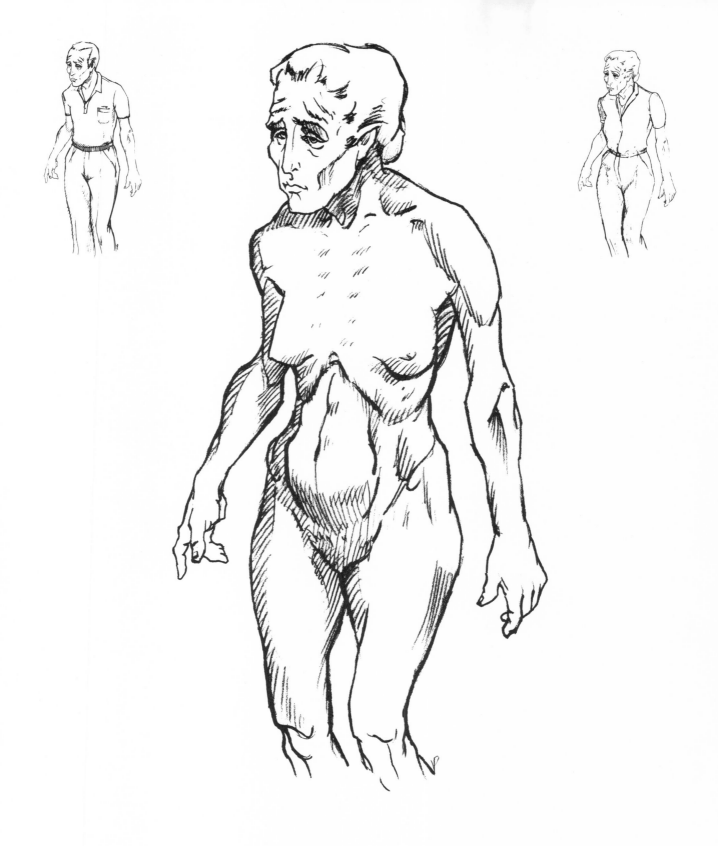

107 EMOTIONAL STANCE: "USE ME"

IMAGE ONE HUNDRED AND EIGHT. Direction of force: the collapsed structure. The collapsed structure has a weakened muscle function. He appears to lack bones or muscles. His tubes sag. The arrows show pressure inward and downward like gravity pulling a mass down by its own weight. The spinal muscles are weak. The digestive tube collapses. The diaphragm flattens and the chest sinks into the exhalation position. Inspiration becomes effortful. He is a belly breather. As the brain sags, excitation becomes minimized. The clavicle constriction implodes and results in a feeling of drowning. The pelvic implosion produces a protrusion as if the abdomen were falling outward. This structure has little ability to withstand pressure. His pouches cave in and the lower pelvic world becomes a pool or swamp.

Viewed as a tube, the collapsed structure appears empty. Pouches sag and protrude. The container wall is limp. The peristaltic wave is aborted because it is not able to overcome downward drag. The excitatory wave compresses.

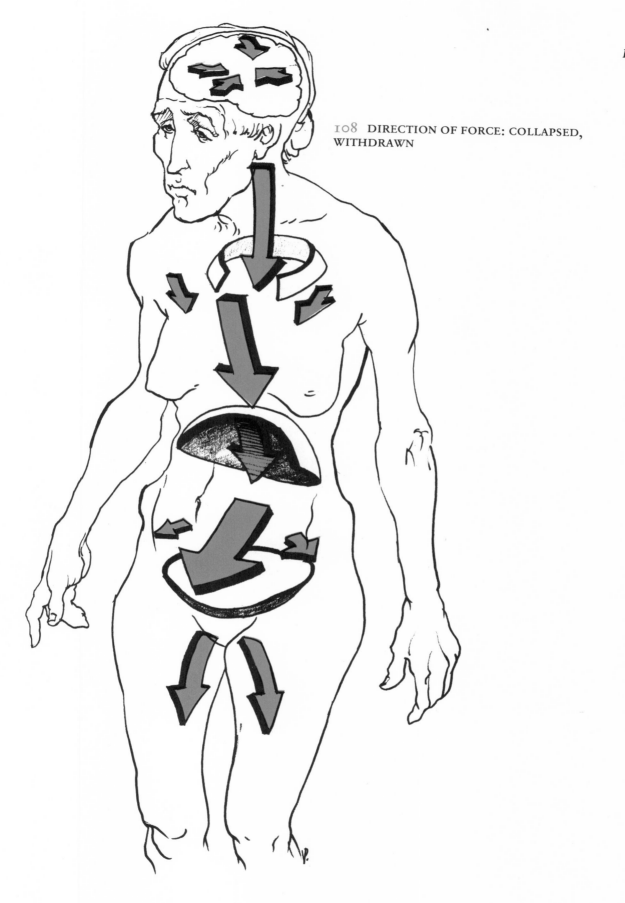

108 DIRECTION OF FORCE: COLLAPSED,
WITHDRAWN

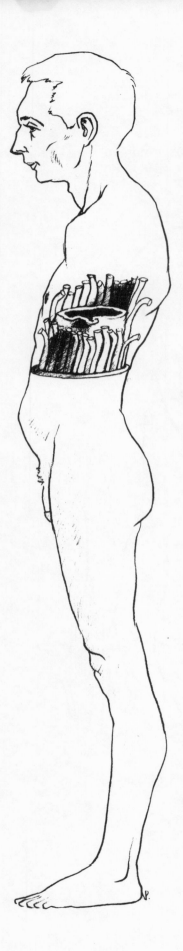

IMAGE ONE HUNDRED AND NINE. The collapsed tube as a body form. In the collapsed structure the muscle wall, spinal cord, and internal tubes are weak. The inner core lacks structure and falls in on itself rather than outward. This structure is unable to firm up or stiffen. When tubes have no support, they collapse. Pulsation dies down as the organism retreats to a lower level of functioning. This structure displays weakness and fear.

109 A COLLAPSED TUBE AS A BODY FORM

IMAGE ONE HUNDRED AND TEN. Collapsed uprightness and the anti-gravitational muscles. The outer wall of the collapsed person sags downward. The abdomen protrudes. The oblique and quadratus femoris muscles thin out. The compensating contractions of the neck muscles prevent the head from rolling around or falling on the chest. The occipital muscles become spastic. The scalene and sternocleidomastoid muscles overstretch. The trapezius muscles contract strongly. The muscles of the chest wall are weak causing a deep kyphosis in the thoracic spine. The chest sinks. Nothing can move through the organism, as it is braced to keep from falling either inward or down. The lungs and heart sag downward. The organism has little inclination to fill up.

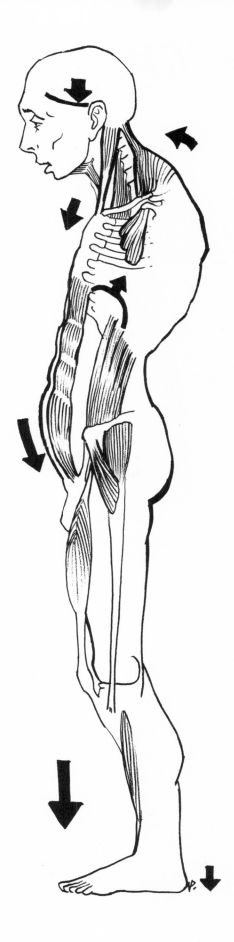

110 ANTI-GRAVITY STANCE: COLLAPSED, SINKING IN, RESIGNED

IMAGE ONE HUNDRED AND ELEVEN. Pump function: the collapsed structure. The pouches in the collapsed person are weak and passive; thus, they fail to maintain an excitatory state. The collapsed person maintains his excitation in his digestive tubes, top brain, and brain stem. Excitation gets dissipated.

All collapsed pouches sag and protrude in a downward direction. It is as if all the inner spaces fell inward. When pouches collapse there is little tidal action. With little pumping up and down, the accordion-like function is minimized. Feelings of emptiness, despair, yielding, and submissiveness result. There is shallow movement in all the diaphragms. Each pouch fuses into the next. Internal movement is felt as sinking. Only the powerful tensions at the base of the skull keep the collapsed structure from falling inward.

III COLLAPSED PUMP FUNCTION: SHRINKING

IMAGE ONE HUNDRED AND TWELVE. Collapse as a pattern of over-contraction. Dynamic forces interrupt excitatory flows, peristaltic pulsations, and organ motility. In this image black areas symbolize dense tissue, a lack of motility or excitation. White areas show excitation that is active and free-flowing. Striped areas show both excitation and constriction—areas that are both active and inactive. Finally, the arrows in the image indicate the direction of muscle pull or pressure.

The dynamics of depression, despair, and weakness are found in the collapsed structure. The organs of energy generation are dark, indicating lack of excitation in contrast with the striped areas of the chest and brain. This structure lacks motility and excitation. The inner tubes are stiffened while the general tube is collapsed. The shoulders are sunken as if carrying a great weight.

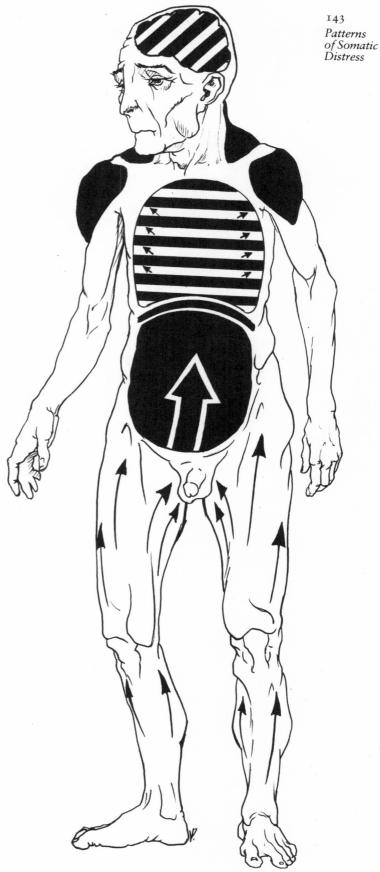

somatic shape and behavioral expression

IMAGE ONE HUNDRED AND THIRTEEN
conveys a total picture of the collapsed
structure and dynamics and illustrates:

- the layering principle;
- the internal and external dynamics and
  how they are related;
- the pouch and diaphragm principle—
  pouches can be pulled out of or pushed
  into their adjoining pouch with resulting
  affects on motility and peristalsis;
- the direction of forces of the total
  structure—out of the pelvis, off of the
  ground or into the pelvis, anchored to
  the ground;
- the configuration of the internal tubes.

Each image presents a different aspect of the
structure.

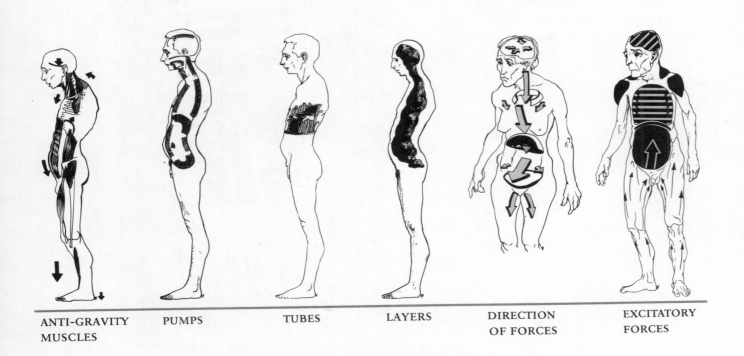

ANTI-GRAVITY   PUMPS   TUBES   LAYERS   DIRECTION   EXCITATORY
MUSCLES   OF FORCES   FORCES

113   COLLAPSED PATTERNS

They fantasize yet dare not dream for fear
   of awakening.
Aloneness is their pain yet they do not give
   to others.
Their mark is empathy.
Their goal is not love but to be taken care
   of.
They fear detachment but they are
   rejectors.
To want is to die.
They avoid the cold but do not burn.

ROLES
Skeptical
Detached

APPEARANCE
Sunken down
Caved in
Formless
Unshaped

STATES OF MIND
Disinterested
Living in fantasy
Apathetic

FEELINGS/EMOTIONAL QUALITIES
Obedient
Hollow
Disappointed
Weak
Unappreciated
Sympathetic
Receptive
Resentful
Cheated
Despairing
Resigned
Abandoned
Victimized
Non-theatening
Unassuming
Ineffective

FEARS
Being big
Hostility
Helplessness
Lack of support
Being controlled
Being detached
Lack of response

TRADITIONAL PSYCHOLOGICAL CATEGORIES
Borderline
Oral-dependent
Depressive

PSYCHOLOGICAL FUNCTIONING
Agitated withdrawal
Listless clinging
Waiting to be
   approached
Seeking love and
   union
Crying to be taken
   care of
Conflicted between
   being alone and
   needing others

EXCITATION
Detached
Under-excited
Deadened
Soft

MOTILITY
Subdued
Weakly bounded
Poorly formed
Unable to stiffen

RELATIONSHIP TO GROUND
Pooled into
Part of background
Collapsed

POUCHES
Imploded
Caved in

EXPERIENCES SELF
In inner layers,
   internal muscles of
   abdomen, lumbar
   spine, pelvis,
   cranial vault and
   spine
Upper half of torso as
   sagging

BODY STANCE
Sagging head
Weakened neck
Collapsed chest
Dense shoulders
Depressed diaphragm
Sagging abdomen
Protruding pelvis

BASIC CHARACTERISTICS
Sympathy
Emotional
   nourishment
Seeking aliveness

RELATES TO OTHERS
Get other into him
Detached
Apathetic

FIGHT STYLE
Appeasement
Accommodation
Power through
   submission

AUTHORITY RELATIONSHIP
Yields
Seeks support
Obedient, slavish
Needs to be led
"Help me do it"

AT WORK
Forms alliances
Non-dominating
Receptive
Not productive

PEER/SUBORDINATE RELATIONSHIP
Accepting
Detached
Meets others' needs
Resists control
Tolerates others'
   weaknesses

RELATES TO SPOUSE, CHILDREN
Affectionate
Yields under stess
Fears abandonment,
   clings
Uses excitement for
   contact
Plays helpless

SEXUAL FUNCTIONING
Needs other to arouse
Lacks sexual assertion
Pelvis is minimally
   responsive

SOMATIC EDUCATION AND CLINICAL DIRECTION
Inflate
Make upright
Encourage desire
Encourage self-esteem
Build inner support
   structure using
   connective tissue
Build rhythmicity,
   encourage
   excitation
Help to control self,
   take pressure
Restore pulsatory
   vitality

structural comparisons

The following overviews compare the four structures as to what effect pressure and motility have on pouches, vertical peristalsis, excitatory flow, circumferential forces; how distress distorts the tube and pouches either from inside out or outside in; and how the stress pattern reflects a pattern of defense.

IMAGE ONE HUNDRED AND FOURTEEN. Emotional expressions: expanding versus contracting.

 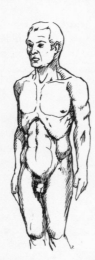 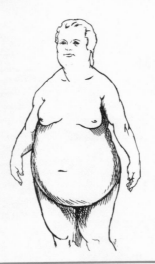 

RIGID
OBEDIENT
CONTROLLED

DENSE
DEFIANT
SHAMED

SWOLLEN
INVASIVE
MANIPULATIVE

COLLAPSED
COMPLIANT
COMPROMISING

IMAGE ONE HUNDRED AND FIFTEEN. Direction of forces—pulled out of the pelvis and off of the ground or pushed into the pelvis and anchored to the ground.

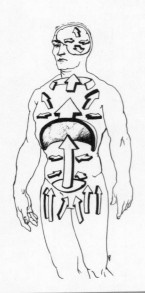  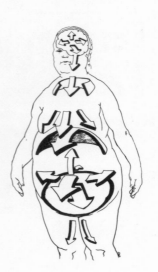 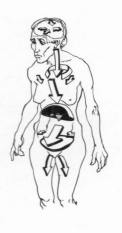

IMAGE ONE HUNDRED AND SIXTEEN. Tube
dynamics and internal effect.

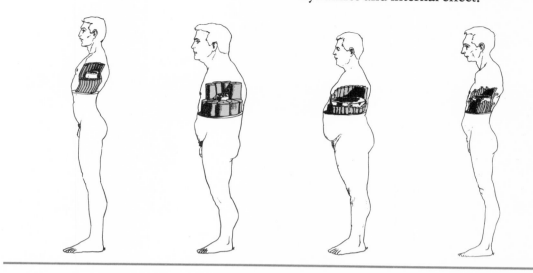

IMAGE ONE HUNDRED AND SEVENTEEN.
Uprightness and the anti-gravitational
muscles.

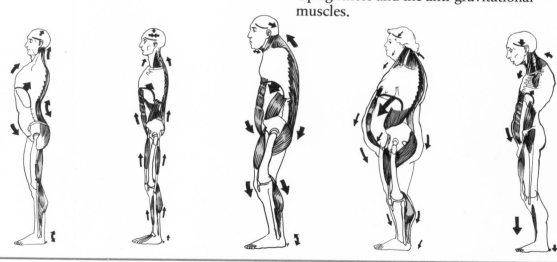

IMAGE ONE HUNDRED AND EIGHTEEN. Pouch dynamics—pulled out of or pushed into adjoining pouches with effects on peristalsis.

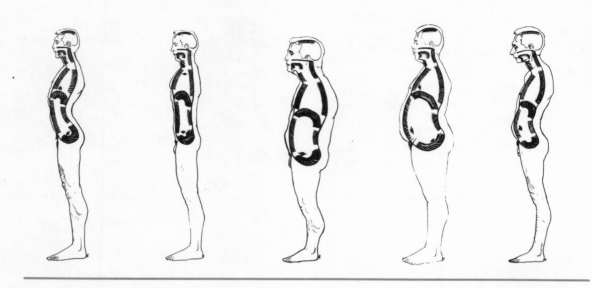

IMAGE ONE HUNDRED AND NINETEEN. Areas of high, low, and conflicted excitation.

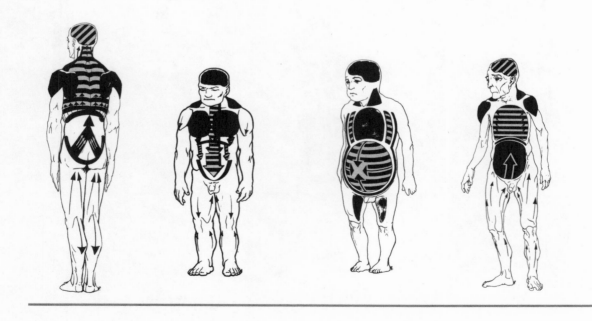

five

somatic reality

HUMAN BEINGS are complex emotional configurations. There is no perfect form, ideal type, or one structure that is better than any other. The shapes seen throughout this book are the consequences of human attempts to love and be loved. They represent the fulfillment or the betrayal of individual attempts to be human, to have control, to be cooperative. Shape also represents the immediate present, how we view the world and try to interact with it for contact, intimacy, and accomplishment.

The history of an individual's emotional experience can be found in tubes, layers, and pouches. Impulses growing out of the pulsatory depths pass through layers to reach the surface for communication and satisfaction. So do stimuli from the outer world pass through the layers of our personal history to reach our depths. Early or late emotional traumas can congeal or freeze one layer of tubes, but this can be overlaid or compensated for by another layer of tightness. An inflated sense of self may cover up the hurt of feeling small.

The organism's emotional layering can be compared to the rings of a tree, each ring revealing age and experience. For example, defiance and pride may cover fear and sadness which in turn cover timidity and anxieties about abandonment. Each of these configurations is somatically structured. The outer layer may be stiff and rigid to cover withdrawal and contraction which further covers the inflated expectation of an abandoned child who fears collapse. These examples illustrate the complexity of somatic reality.

In actual life, somatic reality combines layers and segments to make emotional logic for a particular person. Each of us responds uniquely to the insults and challenges we have to face at different periods in our lives. Our somatic structure is a collage with a thread of continuity that gives to each of us our mark of distinctiveness and individuality.

Some individuals are predominantly rigid, dense, swollen, or collapsed. Many others are combinations of these types, at different layers, in different pouches, or as an upper body-lower body split. Layers and pouches organized to resist continual insults may also have compensatory layers and pouches.

For example, structures unbound at the surface will have overbound compensations deeper in. An over-excited head may be a compensation for an under-excited pelvis. Rigid viscera may compensate for weak muscles. Thus, individuals may not fit neatly into one of the four categories, but their layers and pouches do.

Understanding somatic shape, then, requires the ability to ascertain what somatic configuration is dominant, what other combinations may be present, what layers or pouches are involved, how they affect the person somatically and emotionally, and what visions, perceptions, and self-images they evoke.

IMAGE ONE HUNDRED AND TWENTY. Somatic Reality: the layers and pouches of over-bound and underbound combinations.

RIGID OUTER
DENSE INNER

DENSE OUTER
RIGID INNER

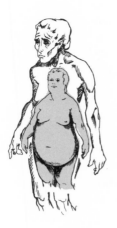

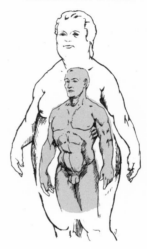

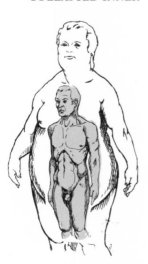

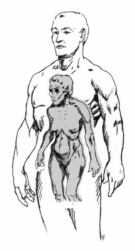

**COLLAPSED OUTER
SWOLLEN INNER**

**SWOLLEN OUTER
COLLAPSED INNER**

**DENSE OUTER
COLLAPSED INNER**

**SWOLLEN OUTER
RIGID INNER**

**SWOLLEN OUTER
DENSE INNER**

**RIGID OUTER
COLLAPSED INNER**

Somatic structure reflects the rules for closeness and distance, tenderness and assertion learned in the family of origin. Insults and shocks, stress and distress are imprinted on every cell, creating a somatic, emotional, psychological image that is enmeshed with all the associated events of life. Insults disturb the continuum of peristaltic pulsations and organize states that are solid-like (rigid or dense) or liquid-like (swollen or collapsed) as a total structure or at different layers and pouches. Ill-formed, unformed, or overformed shapes take on the feelings and limitations which accompany the shape. Action becomes limited. We fear either losing control or being in control. We lose flexibility and the ability for self-management. The interchange among the variety of roles that establishes ego strength is lost. Somatic education and reorganization, therefore, address all these dimensions—pulsation, structure, thinking, feeling, linking head to heart, and soma to soul.

This chapter establishes some basic dimensions of somatic education or formativeness. Formativeness refers to how an individual uses the understandings of somatic structure in self-management. At the same time, this chapter gives clues to those whose profession it is to help others. Although this is not primarily a remedial book, it does present a general way of looking at the somatic archetypes of each personality.

The ability to turn pulsation into peristalsis, and peristalsis into pumping is at the base of healthy physical, emotional, mental, sexual, and interpersonal functioning. This ability gives the basic emotional language of feeling from which movement and expression grow. Distress creates contractions or weaknesses that distort pulsation. Somatic education brings people into deeper contact with the living foundations of existence, the pulsatory waves that generate excitement, feeling, thinking, and action.

While there are many somatic techniques available in the marketplace, not all of them are appropriate for any given individual. Mechanical and cathartic movements, pumped-up breathing techniques, general excitatory exercises, sensory awareness, reposturing and repatterning motor skills, dance movement, psychodrama, and grounding exercises must be viewed in terms of individual differences in structure. Relaxing muscles will not create emotional responsiveness in rigid structures. Breathing approaches or cathartic exercises will not help swollen unbound types. Reposturing the collapsed person will not develop his inner motility. Each structure must be approached uniquely. Emotional misery results for many people when they attempt to become someone else's somatic ideal.

The categories of rigid, dense, swollen, and collapsed do not indicate psychopathology, mental disorder, or physical disease. Neither are they a simplified typology into which all people can be put. What they represent is somatic reality—the interaction between the genetic given and a personal emotional history reflected in our shape and the way we function in thinking, feeling, and action.

IMAGE ONE HUNDRED AND TWENTY-ONE.
The rigid structure.

Rigid structures grow up in families that inhibit pulsation and feeling. They make the child fight for what he wants, demand he be aggressive, and punish displays of tenderness. The result is that aggression dominates tenderness. When a rigid structure can soften, he comes down toward the ground and pelvis. Feelings of sadness, longing, and crying may emerge. Tenderness can then be balanced with assertion.

In the rigid structure the upward excitatory rush involves a conflict of forces. While the rigid builds up potential energy to frighten others away, he also becomes ungrounded and off balance. The inner organs pull upward and backward. Pressure, as indicated by the arrows, should be reversed. The major constriction points are around the clavicle and pubic area as well as the lower ribs and diaphragm.

The lower pouch compresses while the upper pouch swells and inflates. As the chest pulls upward and backward, it creates pressure on the throat resulting in a feeling of being closed or choking. The pelvic muscular ring narrows and results in another constricted exit.

The lower body has to rejoin the top. To restore the integrity of the pouches, the muscle wall needs to learn to swell and elongate. As internal pressure diminishes, horizontal, vertical, and circumferential motility increases. The deep contractions of the neck, head, and lumbar spine need to elongate and lengthen.

One objective is to keep excitation in a rigid structure disciplined rather than letting it act out explosively. Working at the pelvic basin, the psoas, lower rib cage, lumbar and abdominal muscles helps excitation reverse course and run downward, re-establishing a visceral-abdominal state. This reverses both the upper direction of excitation and the excessive narrowing of the lower pouches.

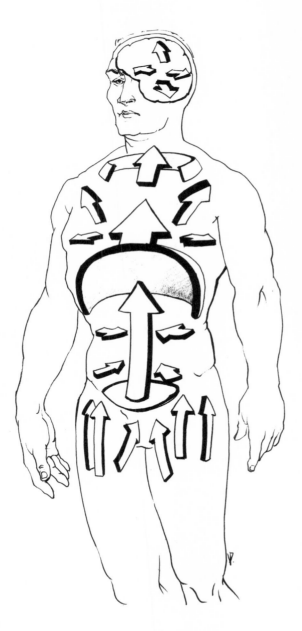

IMAGE ONE HUNDRED AND TWENTY-TWO. The dense structure.

Dense structures come from families that crush pulsation with promises and betrayal, humiliation and doubt. They wish the child to be a slave and never gain independence. Tenderness dominates assertion, choking it off.

For the dense structure the restoration of pulsation is essential. When this person can elongate and reverse his compactedness, he can restore the integrity and separation of the pouches and diminish internal pressure.

Elongation is the key: to stretch the legs, elongate the torso, separate the compactedness of the chest from the pelvis, and hyper-extend the spine. This process of elongating the shortening or contractive reflex strengthens the natural elongation-contraction function. The muscle sheath then functions as a wave instead of a cramp. When the surface area increases, the neck and head lengthen and separate. When the pressure on the outer wall releases, excitation comes to the surface and elongates the organism.

The dense tube needs to pulsate, the head and neck to connect, and the neck to elongate from the torso so that the inner fires can reach the surface. With dense structures, it is important to encourage assertion, link expansion with self-confidence, and link assertion with pleasure. Pulsation overcomes pressure build-up and generates feelings that may have been repressed.

IMAGE ONE HUNDRED AND TWENTY-THREE. The swollen structure.

Swollen structures grow up in families that are excitable, seductive, and manipulative. Emphasis is on closeness and merging. Swollen structures can learn to make distance and establish boundaries by compressing and strengthening the abdominal wall, inflating the chest and separating it from the abdomen, and creating inner pressure to restore a tidal action. As shown by the direction of the arrows, the swollen person pours out rather than contains himself. This outpouring differs from the eruption of the rigid type or the implosion of the dense. The swollen structure, unlike the rigid or dense, cannot take great pressure from outside in or inside out. Pressure creates deflation.

Vertical motility and pressure are re-established by learning inhibition and reversing outer excitation which has congealed on the surface. As the chest pouch expands, longitudinal waves of pulsation overcome this side pressure. It is essential for swollen structures to learn compression.

Inner motility is learned as the surface constricts, and, at the same time, the head tension releases. As this structure empties, it caves into a proper size, rebuilding on a deflated but not collapsed self. As boundaries rebuild there is an increase in feeling and excitement. For the swollen type, containment, shrinking and building up the inner spaces give the sense of an interior life.

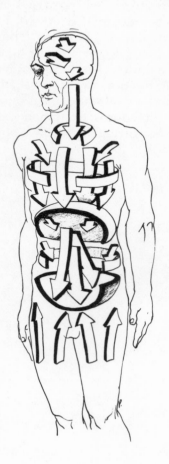

122 THE DENSE STRUCTURE

The collapsed structure.
    Families that abandon, show indifference, or diminish their children often produce collapsed structures. These structures cannot fill up or fill out, and now seek substance and the arousal of their fires of excitation.

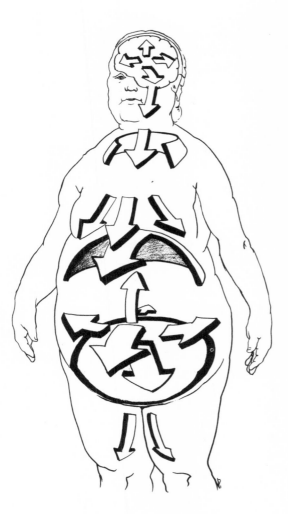

123   **THE SWOLLEN STRUCTURE**

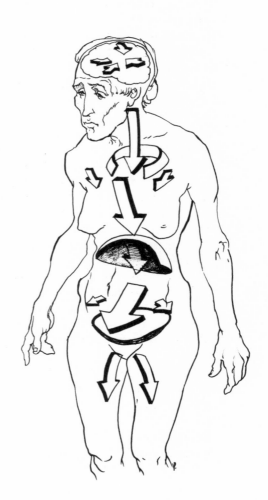

124   **THE COLLAPSED STRUCTURE**

In order to increase vertical peristalsis and to increase motility and excitation, collapsed structures need to feel their bones, stimulate pulsation in their internal organs, and inflate their inner pouches. As motility increases and inner pressure builds, a flow of excitation begins. Pressure is the key to motility in all the tubes. To inspire, to force breathing, to take action, to face challenge, to become firm—all are necessary. The head raises up, lifting the chest, and excitation of bone tissue calls for muscle stiffening in response to gravity.

With collapsed structures, the tension in the muscle wall remains undisturbed until an inner vitality of organ pulsations and oxygenation can act as an inner force to buoy up or inflate the person. The person needs an inner charge that demands outer muscle reorganization. If this is accompanied by feelings of moving and structure, this person can begin to elongate, pull himself up, and acquire impulses that seek support from the muscles or the bones.

An increase in respiration and rhythmical motions provokes excitation and the flooding of sensations as well as peristaltic pulsations. This results in an internal growth, stimulation of the oral and respiratory tubes, and a general filling out. The weight will be lifted from the shoulders, thus, there can be fuller inspiration. The structure fills up. Hope is re-kindled.

Thus, reorganization differs for the overbound and underbound structures. Rigid and dense structures are powerfully expansive or deeply contracted to quell fear or to prevent loss of control. As deeper levels are destructured, the doors open to the well-springs of desire and feeling. On the other hand, collapsed and swollen types need restructuring, not destructuring. Boundaries have to be established and pouch separation defined. Restoration of the pulsatory, accordion-like function differs according to the structure. With the overbound the disorganization of layers of contraction does not result in collapse. But in the underbound, abrupt removal of contractions risks disorganization and severe problems.

In structures which are a mixture of overbound and underbound the corrective action indicated for the rigid, dense, swollen, or collapsed applies to separate layers or individual pouches.

Somatic education and reorganization require a dialogue among compartments and layers so that pulsation has a continuity that communicates between inside and outside, from brain stem to thalamus to cortex, from excitement and feeling to understanding and action. Contact with the self, to really experience one's self, is the first step. Then it is necessary to bring to the foreground the basic states of pulsation, their feelings and expression that restore faith in one's self. But, most importantly, one must disorganize and restructure the pulsatory reflexes of expansion and contraction together with the emotional components of pleasure, anger, sadness and crying, filling up and emptying. Maximum satisfaction lies, not in perpetuating one set of fixated actions and feelings, but in the ability to be firm, withhold, swell up, yield and retreat as alternative responses, any of which may be appropriate to the exigencies of daily life.

six

somatic interactions

ANATOMICAL STRUCTURE is the basic arche-
type of thought and experience. Anatomy is
internal relationship. Organs relate to other
organs, layers of specialized tissue are in
relationship with other layers, surfaces contact other surfaces. Anatomical relationships
are also emotional relationships. Pulsating
organs generate good feeling, a sense of well-
being, pleasure. Constricted, spastic, bloated
or weak tissue gives rise to pain, discomfort,
unpleasant feelings about one's self or a part
of one's self. Anatomy and feeling are also
behavioral relationships. Any breakdown in
anatomical or emotional organization
results in an equivalent breakdown in
behavior.

Anatomy is the foundation for human
relationship. What happens in our interior,
those connections that maintain the structure of personhood, eventually happens outside as well. Pulsation and its shape is the
cornerstone of organismic process as well as
intrapersonal and interpersonal forms.
Human relationships are somatic interactions of emotional pulsation and behavioral
form—inside us, outside us.

We relate to others via the forms we make.
If we become rigid, dense, or unyielding,
we may find ourselves spitefully or fearfully
withdrawn. We are unable to reach out or to
empathize with others. If we deny our feelings and needs or hide our desires, we may
seek out people who also act only out of

frustration or who have little interest in their lives. This frustration and resignation become an organismic state of mind as well as our self-reference.

Of course, what happens outside also affects what goes on inside. If we are disregarded or alienated by society, we may shrink into despair and feel unworthy. We may also get stiff with pride and indignation or feel ourselves superior to our antagonists even while rigidity covers our hurt. The opposite is also true. As we inwardly destructure rigidities and allow internal pulsation to again become peristaltic, we reach out to engage others. This enhances self-image and creates good feeling as the basis of arousal. If people accept us and value our contributions, we join them and disorganize the pride that creates distance. Acceptance by others enriches us, creates hope and feelings about a future.

Life's emotional experiences create form and shape. Shape gives emotions, thinking, feeling an avenue for expression and satisfaction or the opposite, inhibition and pain. With our shape we interact with the world and create relationships. As we reach out to others for contact, love, intimacy, cooperation, we may create relationships that serve to reinforce or compensate for our individual shape.

IMAGE ONE HUNDRED AND TWENTY-FIVE. Somatic interactions. Human relationships are a dynamic emotional process sustaining and expressing morphology.

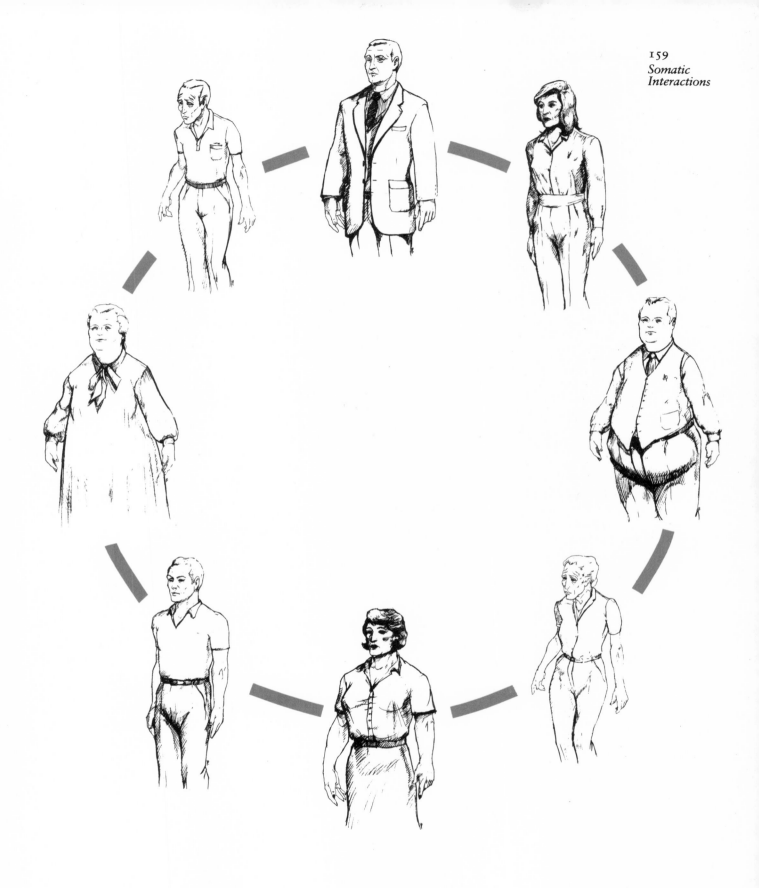

Each of us faces another. This other interacts with us, provides responses to our actions and, in turn, provokes responses from us. Our basic humanity depends upon this feeling of connection. A bond is established through a system of powerful connections —body surfaces, language, eyes, feeling, emotional intimacy, love, and sexuality.

Love and intimacy are the wellsprings of human endeavor. We touch each other from the wells of desire and the labyrinths of memories of early caring—success or failure at loving and being loved. Depth, inwardness, and union begin a bond which melts layers of caution and fear, bravado and longing as we share somatic truth.

IMAGE ONE HUNDRED AND TWENTY-SIX.
Coupling: The layering of emotional connection.

Contact with others is more than surface to surface, it is also inside to inside. Contact is layered, from the outer skin surfaces of communication to the second layer of gesture and action, to the third layer of visceral motility. Contact, vulnerability, and intimacy involve these surface and depth interactions.

The outer layer concerns the shape by which we are recognized and the social roles we play. Inner layers contain instinctual statements, statements of desire, need, and hunger emanating from the deepest layer of the visceral self. On another layer, these stances are emotional statements of softness and firmness, receptivity and distance, collapse and rigidity.

Love and intimacy change emotional expression by permitting the experiences that lower defenses. This permits a taste, if only briefly, of tender satisfaction. Over time, as love and intimacy continue and develop, appropriate shapes are formed. As pulsation becomes more rhythmical and warmly compelling, a communion is organized. From the depths, layer by layer, new somatic shapes emerge.

To live somatic-emotional truth means to contact an inner image that wells up from the somatic depths, from the basic pulsatile inheritance that gives rise to cycles of action, thought, feeling. Knowing one's self somatically is not only muscular, emotional, biochemical, sensorial awareness, but is also the organization of excitation represented in the visible and invisible peristaltic waves of our living selves.

Look again at the images throughout this book. They do not present bodies in the usual sense of that word. They present emotional anatomy, a dynamic process of living forms and individual shapes that are ourselves, universally and personally, the process of life with an outer and inner, public and private existence. This is what health and wholeness, stress and disease, transitions and crises, conflicts and resolution, love and fulfillment really mean—human beings organizing an existence.

Anatomy is destiny as long as it is a somatic process. We must learn to re-envision anatomy more than as a static materialism, more than pictures of the dead, abstractions in the form of physiological formulas, ideas about nature rather than nature itself. Anatomy is really about a dynamic living process, a mystery, an initiation, the shape of experience which gives rise to feeling, thought, and action. It is about ourselves as feeling forms. It is about genetic, embryological, and personal history. It is about the insults we received from our families and society and what we did to preserve our own integrity under duress. Anatomy really concerns the form we were given by nature, the forms we had to create as part of a particular society and family, and the form we are presently shaping. To know emotional anatomy is to experience the pains of desire and disappointment, the conflicts of contact and the striving for satisfaction, the taste of intimacy and individuality, the knowledge of conditional and unconditional love.

126 COUPLING: THE LAYERS OF
EMOTIONAL-ANATOMICAL CONNECTION

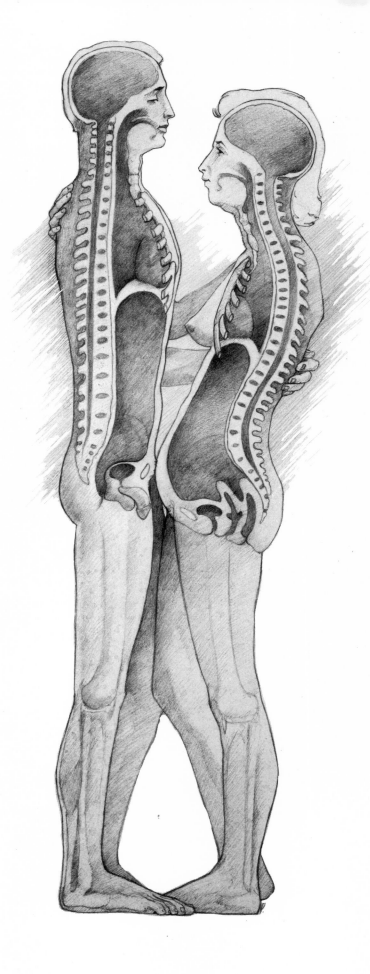

also by Stanley Keleman

In Defense of Heterosexuality (1982)
Somatic Reality (1979)
Your Body Speaks Its Mind (1975)
Living Your Dying (1974)
Human Ground:
    Sexuality, Self, and Survival (1971)
Todtmoos: A Book of Poems (1971)

center for energetic studies

The Center for Energetic Studies, under the direction of Stanley Keleman, seeks to structure a modern contemplative approach to self-knowing and living in which one's own subjective process gives birth to a set of values which then guides the whole of one's life. Today's values are increasingly divorced from our deepest processes, and bodily experience has been misunderstood and relegated to second place.

Somatic reality is an emotional reality that is much larger than innate genetic patterns of behavior. Emotional reality and biological ground are the same and cannot, in any way, be separated or distinguished. Biological ground also means gender, the male and female responses that are innate to human life, the sexual identity with which we are born. Somatic reality is at the very core of exsistence, the source of our deepest religious feelings and psychological perceptions.

Classes and programs at the Center offer a psycho-physical practicum that brings to use the basic ways a person learns. The key issue is *how* we use ourselves—learning the language of how viscera and brain use muscle to create behavior. These classes teach the essential somatic aspect of all roles and dramatize the possibilities of action to deepen the sense of connection to the many worlds in which all of us participate.

For further information, write to:
Center for Energetic Studies
2045 Francisco Street
Berkeley, California 94709